As Terrorism Evolves

Some of the world's most lethal terrorist organizations have become media-centric enterprises, while also hijacking a major world religion, holding large swaths of physical territory, and governing their own virtual states. In this concise and penetrating book, Seib traces how terrorism has proliferated and increased significantly in menace in the relatively brief period between the rise of Al Qaeda and the creation of Islamic State. With close attention to the linkages between media, religion, and violence, the book offers incisive analysis of how organizations such as Islamic State, Al Qaeda, and Boko Haram operate and reflects on how terrorism may continue to evolve. Seib argues that twenty-first-century terrorism is enabled by new media and depends on social networks as connective tissue, while interacting with religion and socioeconomic and political grievances. An indispensable resource for students and knowledgeable nonspecialists, *As Terrorism Evolves* prescribes new measures for counterterrorism efforts, underscores the importance of soft power, and makes a strong case for recognizing that we have entered an era of terrorism of undetermined duration.

PHILIP SEIB is one of the world's leading authorities on the intersection of media and foreign policy. A frequent visitor to the Middle East, he has examined Arab politics in books such as *The Al Jazeera Effect* (2008) and *Real-Time Diplomacy* (2012). Seib is Professor of Journalism, Public Diplomacy, and International Relations at the University of Southern California and was named International Communication Distinguished Scholar by the International Studies Association. He is author and editor of more than two dozen books and writes frequently for the *Huffington Post* about terrorism and international politics. His interest in terrorism was piqued when he found himself just forty miles from Mosul as that city was being seized by Islamic State in 2014.

As Terrorism Evolves

Media, Religion, and Governance

PHILIP SEIB

University of Southern California

CAMBRIDGE
UNIVERSITY PRESS

CAMBRIDGE
UNIVERSITY PRESS

University Printing House, Cambridge CB2 8BS, United Kingdom

One Liberty Plaza, 20th Floor, New York, NY 10006, USA

477 Williamstown Road, Port Melbourne, VIC 3207, Australia

4843/24, 2nd Floor, Ansari Road, Daryaganj, Delhi – 110002, India

79 Anson Road, #06-04/06, Singapore 079906

Cambridge University Press is part of the University of Cambridge.

It furthers the University's mission by disseminating knowledge in the pursuit of education, learning, and research at the highest international levels of excellence.

www.cambridge.org
Information on this title: www.cambridge.org/9781108411691
DOI: 10.1017/9781108303996

First published 2017

Printed in the United Kingdom by Clays, St Ives plc

A catalogue record for this publication is available from the British Library.

ISBN 978-1-108-41970-3 Hardback
ISBN 978-1-108-41169-1 Paperback

He was a force. His thoughts caressed the images of ruin and destruction ... Nobody looked at him. He passed on unsuspected and deadly, like a pest in the street full of men.

Joseph Conrad, *The Secret Agent*, 1906

Contents

Preface

Writing about terrorism is challenging in several ways.

First, it is terribly depressing to survey the destruction that terrorists cause – so many lives destroyed, so much progress reversed. Describing all this is like wading into a fetid swamp from which there seems little chance of escape. This extends to getting to know the terrorists. Some in the lower ranks are just foolishly misguided, but most in these organizations are thugs who seek to justify their behavior by wrapping it in flimsy religiosity.

Also, incidents of outrage occur so frequently that for anyone trying to paint on as broad a canvas as a book, it is hard to keep up. Besides the never-ending attacks, new terrorist groups emerge, new tactics are employed by and against them, and new approaches to counterterrorism are unveiled.

What quickly becomes clear is that twenty-first-century terrorism is, unfortunately, more than a short-lived aberration. Its continuing evolution is the principal theme of this book, and its staying power is growing. Terrorist organizations will have their ups and downs, but they have proved to have survival skills that will sustain them for the foreseeable future. And as Islamic State has shown, terrorists can emerge from their caves and take control of large swathes of territory, perhaps not permanently but long enough to bring the world's great powers into the fight. Further, they can set up governance structures with income generated by everything from extortion to oil production.

So, where are we going with all this? What will post–Islamic State terrorism be like? The blending of insurgency in a defined area with terror attacks globally is frightening enough today, but other extremists are watching Islamic State and learning from its successes and failures. Al Qaeda, for instance, has been reshaping and rebuilding itself while letting Islamic State be the primary counterterrorism target, and it is poised to build its own caliphate on the rubble Islamic State leaves behind.

All this matters because, in one way or another, terrorism touches all our lives. As we step into a street market in Baghdad or a nightclub in Istanbul, a cloud of worry accompanies us. At an airport in Los Angeles or Paris, we complain about security procedures although we recognize their necessity. While sitting in a movie theater or walking through a shopping mall, we glance at the exits as we recall incidents when someone sprayed gun fire in a public place.

We all literally pay a price for terrorism, with vast amounts of money being directed into counterterrorism programs and military buildups instead of being devoted to education, medical research, or other priorities that would improve our lives.

How we react to terrorism, a phenomenon we do not truly understand, is another matter for concern. Egged on by irresponsible political leaders, some of us lash out at entire groups of people. About 1.6 billion Muslims live around the world, of which only the tiniest percentage engages in violence, and yet terrorism- (and immigration-) related Islamophobia is on the rise. This widening cultural divide obstructs efforts to deal with terrorism and build a constructive civil society.

All these matters served as motivation for writing this book. I hope its readers will see that countering terrorism requires embracing reason, and that well-structured knowledge should prevail over facile emotionalism.

Journalists, historians, religion scholars, and many others have written much about the issues addressed in this book, and I thank them all. (Some of their work is listed in the Select Bibliography at the end of this volume.) More directly, two young scholars, Gozde Kurt and Noorhan Maamoon, helped me with material about Islam. Maura Conway and Romy Froelich, leaders of important projects that examine radicalization, were kind enough to invite me to work with them. My academic colleagues at the University of Southern California (USC) and the International Studies Association have consistently been supportive. In our class discussions, my USC students provided much for me to think about.

At Cambridge University Press, Sara Doskow was a steadfast believer in this book and helped me immeasurably with her thoughtful suggestions. She has been wonderful to work with. My ever-patient agent, Robbie Anna Hare of Goldfarb and Associates, always offered encouragement.

I want to also recognize those who, in the aftermath of a terrorist attack, rush to save lives of innocents who are victims of the senseless violence. Ambulance teams, police officers, and even passersby provide assistance and comfort at a terrible moment. It is a sad fact that they have become so important, but their work underscores the breadth of the evolving menace of terrorism. Their efforts should not be overlooked.

Introduction

Islamic State (IS) held Mosul, Iraq's second largest city, for the better part of three years, all the while encouraging or orchestrating terror attacks in Europe and elsewhere. Its "capital" – Raqqa, Syria – functioned even longer, despite persistent attacks from some of the world's most powerful nations.

Consider what that means in terms of the nature of terrorism. Rather than a singular act, such as the 9/11 attacks in the United States, after which the perpetrators kill themselves, are caught or killed by authorities, or go into hiding, we now have a terrorist organization that seizes substantial amounts of territory, "governs" that territory through a bureaucracy that addresses everything from bomb making to human services, and establishes "provinces" around the world, all the while continuing to spread bloody havoc.

This is the new era of terrorism. The terrorist act has morphed into the terrorist state. It must be understood and confronted.

When an act of terrorism occurs, we – individually and collectively – react with horror, sadness, anger; our responses are grounded in emotion. We then look to law enforcement, the military, and government more broadly to respond, presumably in ways that transcend our own emotional reactions. We expect them to do what is necessary to right the wrong and protect us against further attacks.

Only in rare cases can this latter goal be achieved solely by capturing or killing the perpetrators of a particular attack. Seldom is terrorism the act of a true loner with no ties whatsoever to the global terrorism infrastructure. Even so-called lone-wolf attackers, such as the brothers who committed the 2013 Boston Marathon bombing or the US military officer who went on a rampage at Fort Hood in 2009, are inspired by terrorist voices that flow so constantly through social media and other channels.

This underscores the difficulty of preventing terrorist acts through preemptive intervention. Prospective violent actors sometimes make errors that allow government agencies to spot them and arrest them before they can commit their crimes, but counting on terrorists to be sloppy is not an effective strategy. The extremist universe is vast, and the people at the center of it are as smart as they are ruthless.

The terrorist act is the capstone of a process that builds from a foundation of alienation and anger. It is nurtured by extreme political or religious beliefs combined with vicious criminality and often fortified by content disseminated through online venues. Linkages among violence, religion, and media are at the heart of the evolution of modern terrorism. By examining these factors individually and collectively, this book illustrates how they mutually reinforce one another and make terrorism more difficult to control.

Further, terrorism's evolutionary process must be recognized as such. Today's terrorism has changed significantly from its previous incarnations, and counterterrorism strategies must be adjusted accordingly to keep pace and perhaps even get ahead to the point at which prevention, not merely reaction, is possible.

Terrorism has caused the deaths of many thousands and has terrified millions more. Just as the Cold War, with its threat of nuclear destruction, loomed over the second half of the twentieth century, terrorism has been taking lives and draining resources throughout the first two decades of the twenty-first ... and it is virtually certain to continue and keep evolving in ways that make it more brutish and resilient.

We are in for a nasty ride during the coming years; this book contends that we have entered a "terrorism era" that has no perceptible end date. The scale, level of proliferation, and skill of communicating and networking demonstrated by terrorist organizations is striking.

The initial response to this evil phenomenon was to begin a "global war on terror," which was flawed from the start by its attempt to use conventional methods to deal with an unconventional foe. This was seen in the US response to the 9/11 terrorist attacks of 2001. The American military orchestrated the end (at least temporarily) of Taliban rule in Afghanistan and killed many Al Qaeda fighters. The rest of Al Qaeda, including its top leadership, escaped into Pakistan. The United States, like a boxer swinging wildly, extended its military efforts into Iraq and soon found itself trying to manage unmanageable conflicts in two countries. Despite the death of Osama bin Laden in 2011, Al Qaeda has expanded its operations throughout the Middle East and parts of Africa, and has recently reached into the Indian subcontinent.

By the time Barack Obama's presidency began in 2009, the main goal of the United States in Afghanistan and Iraq was to devise exit strategies. The label "war on terror" was dropped as if it were an outdated commercial logo, and it was replaced by "countering violent extremism" (CVE), which was supposed to differentiate the new administration's approach from that of its predecessor. It implicitly relies on a more holistic view of the problem, recognizing that violent extremism, which in some instances may be more intellectual than kinetic, must be addressed before it gains traction.

Broadening the scope of the response to terrorism in this way makes sense on a theoretical level, but designing a comprehensive CVE campaign that involves more than thrust-and-parry tactics has so far proved to be beyond the abilities of numerous governments that have tried to adopt this approach. CVE is supposed to be linked in a fragile partnership with more conventional counterterrorism efforts that capture or kill those identified as terrorists. (Like terrorism, the terminology describing it also evolves. In late 2016, as the Obama presidency neared its end, CVE was on its way out, with *counterterrorism* once more in vogue ... for the moment.)

Meanwhile, the Al Qaeda franchises in the Middle East were strengthened by the experience their fighters had gained on various battlegrounds and, beginning in 2011, by the new levels of regional instability produced by that year's Arab uprisings. Hopes were initially high that democratic reforms might supersede autocracy and undercut extremists' rhetoric, but except for Tunisia (tenuously), the "Arab spring" produced a new wave of despotism and chaos, and even in Tunisia, thousands of young people became so exasperated by factors such as the lack of economic progress that they left home to join terrorist armies. The hope of 2011 might recover, but for now it is on life support.

Violence is self-nurturing, and a new player that emerged from the detritus of the Iraq War quickly gained a reputation for its military prowess and vicious methods. In June 2014, the previously little-known IS, an offspring of Al Qaeda in Iraq, captured attention when it seized Mosul. IS soon controlled significant parts of Iraq and Syria, proclaiming that its territory superseded the two countries' official borders and constituted the new Islamic caliphate. It financed itself in numerous ways, such as taxing residents of the territory it occupied, exporting oil, and selling looted antiquities. It recruited new fighters and other "citizens" for the caliphate through compulsion, but also through sophisticated use of social media and other tools, its version of "soft power."

At first, it appeared possible to physically contain IS and isolate it as just another "Arab problem." But soon IS took control of parts of Libya and began sponsoring, or at least encouraging, terror attacks far afield. Even as IS suffers battlefield setbacks, it retains the ability to inspire its "soldiers" abroad to attack civilians. As this is written, Beirut, Paris, Brussels, Istanbul, and Nice are among the cities that have been scenes of IS-orchestrated or IS-inspired mass murders.

IS and its kin clearly require a more forceful and imaginative response from Arab states, the broader *ummah* (global Muslim community), and the rest of the world. Reflexive reliance on conventional military methods that involve little risk, such as drone and aircraft attacks, is dangerously naïve. Needed instead is a comprehensive strategy that incorporates a tightly focused military effort along with measures that can alter the political environment in which IS recruitment has flourished. This broad approach is essential to cripple IS and prevent it from giving birth to its own successor.

What might that successor be? My argument throughout this book is that the evolution of terrorism is taking us away from the terrorist cells of old and beyond the traditional structure of early Al Qaeda. We have moved into an era of the terrorist organization not merely as a cadre of like-minded persons or as a state-sponsored enterprise, but rather as a statelike entity.

IS is a prototype of this and, given the rapid evolution of terrorist organization, that is cause for great concern. As of early 2017, the IS grip on territory in Iraq and Syria had been loosened but not broken, and the ability of IS to direct or inspire bloody attacks elsewhere in the world was undiminished. IS had become a two-headed monster: a terrorist organization in the traditional sense of mounting attacks throughout the world, and a military insurgency in terms of taking and holding territory.

Confronting terrorism today means not just dealing with individuals such as Osama bin Laden, but rather requires a more comprehensive strategy to confront the networked terrorist state.

I wrote this book after coming closer to IS attacks than I would have preferred. In June 2014, I happened to be on a research trip (not related to terrorism) in Iraqi Kurdistan, about forty miles from Mosul, when IS first occupied that city. There were many thousands of Kurdish Peshmerga fighters between IS and me, so I could remain fairly calm (as most of the Kurds did) while this hitherto little-known phenomenon took hold. But I soon saw the impact of the IS menace. Iraqi Kurdistan, after many years of abuse at the hands of Saddam Hussein and others, had been flourishing, with new investment in everything from oil to education pointing the region toward prosperity. But the new threat changed all that; military spending sucked up Kurdish resources as the region went onto war footing. This is one of terrorism's ripple effects: Civil society is forced to set aside constructive ambition while it concentrates on defending itself.

Then, in January 2016 in Istanbul, I realized that I had been standing on the exact spot near the Blue Mosque two days before a bomber, identified as an IS operative, set off a bomb there that killed thirteen tourists. This produced a personalized chill; even coincidental proximity to an attack is a reminder that safety is elusive. Also, there were side effects in Turkey – not bloody, but still damaging. The tourism industry that is such an important part of Turkey's economy suffered a significant setback because of this and other terrorist attacks. Terrorism can destroy livelihoods as well as lives.

My own situation on these two occasions was nothing when compared to the horrors inflicted on the citizens of Mosul or the tourists killed in Istanbul. But I was near enough to be reminded that "terrorism" is not an abstraction. Rather, it is a tangible, pervasive evil that must be confronted and brought to an end. My close calls may not have been all that close, but they motivated me to research and write.

A more prosaic reason for writing this book is that I need it for my university teaching. The courses I teach center on foreign policy and media, and terrorism is a topic that comes up frequently. I don't teach a course that is terrorism specific – there are plenty of detailed books for such offerings – but I needed something that could give my students, within a two- or three-week portion of a course, an overview of terrorism issues and how these matters fit into the broader context of international affairs. I have spent much of my academic career examining the connections between media and international relations, and I find it striking how germane this media-oriented focus is today in assessing terrorism. The communication component of terrorism studies continues to become more important.

And so this book is concise, and I hope interesting.

As with many other topics related to current affairs, terrorism does not hold still for analysis. It slithers its way into new identities and atrocities. Although as of early 2017 IS was capturing most terrorism-related headlines, it is far from being the only extremist threat. The US State Department's list of foreign terrorist organizations includes fifty-seven non-IS groups. Most striking is the geographical range of these organizations: Boko Haram in Nigeria; Al Shabaab in Somalia; the Haqqani network in Afghanistan; Jemaah Islamiya in Indonesia; Hamas in Gaza; the Kurdistan Workers Party (PKK) in Turkey; the Real Irish Republican Army; and others scattered across the globe. In the United States, fear and anger about "radical Islamic terrorism" tends to overshadow threats posed by domestic terrorists who have no ties to "radical Islam" but commit their crimes with numbing frequency, as when they kill Planned Parenthood clients in Colorado Springs and police officers in Dallas and Baton Rouge.

There is no "one-size-fits-all" response to individual terrorists and terrorist organizations. Their tactics and degrees of success vary depending on the political and military environments in which they operate, as well as the comparative skills of their own leaders and those who oppose them. What they have in common is their poisonous effect on civil society and the pain they inflict on innocents.

Although violent extremism, in one form or another, has been with us since ancient times, this book focuses on the twenty-first century, which is when the linkages among media, religion, and violence have become so striking and the evolution of terrorism has accelerated. In Chapter 1 we look at the definitions of modern terrorism, of which there are many, propounded by governments and others. As terrorist organizations become more sophisticated and some, such as IS, attain quasistate identities, definitions of *terrorism* may collide with those of *insurgency*, a distinction addressed in the first chapter. The somewhat facile notion that "one person's terrorist is another person's freedom fighter" needs examining, but so does the propensity of some to sweepingly dismiss actions responding to legitimate political grievances as terrorism. Just as terrorism evolves, so too must the terminology used in describing it.

Also in Chapter 1, we examine how terrorism affects our lives and how far we want to go in trying to counter it. Extremist violence today haunts many of us. Who gets on an airplane without eyeing fellow passengers and contemplating scenarios of a hijack or midair explosion? Who shops at a street market in the Middle East or elsewhere without pondering the threat of a suicide bomber? How many democracies feel it appropriate to chip away at individuals' freedoms while trying to protect citizens from terrorists? Such questions illustrate terrorists' ability to insinuate themselves into our personal and community existence. This is the essence of terrorism.

The next step is to analyze the terrorists. What drives men, women, and even children to commit such horrific acts? Many of them have given careful thought to their actions, have specific political or personal ideals they embrace, and are willing to give their lives on behalf of those ideals. As warped as we may consider their behavior to be, there is a logic of sorts that drives these people forward. They must be understood before they can be countered.

Chapter 2 examines the relationship between terrorism and religion. Although not all violent extremism is rooted in religion, and not all terrorists who *are* motivated by religion are Muslims, the connection between many devastating instances of extremism and Islam is a reality that cannot be ignored. This book grapples with that reality, recognizing that it is important in understanding the most pervasive forms of terrorism today and game-changing moments in the evolution of terrorism. That said, stereotyping must be avoided. Muslims worldwide number about 1.6 billion, and by the year 2050 Islam will nearly match Christianity in size. Only a tiny minority of Muslims are violent extremists, but in the view of much of the global public, Muslims' religion is synonymous with the violence perpetrated in Islam's name.

In addressing this connection, Chapter 2 argues that short- and long-term solutions must originate within Islam; measures such as introducing critical thinking into the curricula of *madrasas* have met with success on a small scale, and many imams have urged those who attend their mosques to push back against those who justify violence on religious grounds. The vast majority of Muslims are as horrified as anyone else by terrorist acts. But those Muslims and others who try to use religion in constructive ways find their work complicated by virulent anti-Muslim sentiment that strengthens extremists' case that Islam is under siege.

Chapter 3 focuses on terrorists' organizational skills and makes the case that these continue to mature. Al Qaeda began as vertically organized, with Osama bin Laden issuing directives from the top to his lieutenants and foot soldiers, such as those who participated in the 9/11 attacks against the United States. By the time bin Laden was killed a decade later, Al Qaeda had evolved into more of a network, with "franchises" such as Al Qaeda in the Arabian Peninsula, Al Qaeda in the Islamic Maghreb, and Al Qaeda in the Indian Subcontinent. These groups had enough autonomy that they were little affected by bin Laden's death. Soon thereafter, one of the franchises, Al Qaeda in Iraq, broke away from Al Qaeda and renamed itself IS, also referred to as the Islamic State of Iraq and Syria (ISIS), or the Islamic State of Iraq and the Levant (ISIL), or Da'esh, which is the transliterated Arabic for ISIL. (For simplicity, IS will be used throughout this book except when the other names occur in direct quotes.)

IS's name is far less relevant than is its advanced form of organization. In pursuit of its claim to be a statelike "caliphate," IS developed a civic infrastructure that seeks adherents by providing basic services, purportedly cracking down on corruption, and – most important – offering stability in areas where that has long been unknown. IS also uses sectarianism to its advantage, portraying itself as defender of Sunnis against Shia enemies. It keeps order through a fiercely punitive religiosity, which becomes even more vicious when IS is being battered by its enemies. IS also conducts public diplomacy of sorts through its sophisticated media operations.

Although IS is associated in most people's minds with its grim execution videos, there is far more to it than that. It appeals to Muslim physicians to work in IS hospitals, teachers to work in IS schools, and media experts to present IS to the world (and especially to potential recruits). The message IS sends to many of its target audiences is not "come kill," but rather "Come build the caliphate. Leave behind the life in which you are treated badly because you are a Muslim, and instead join us in defending our faith." The appeal is not unlike the nineteenth-century advice to American pioneers, "Go west, young man, and grow up with the country." IS believes that it, too, has a manifest destiny.

As of this writing in 2017, IS has achieved a considerable level of success. Although it has been attacked by a US-led military coalition, as well as Iranian and Arab forces, it survives and continues to attract recruits from throughout the world. Although intelligence accounts differ, IS seems to be dispersing its fighters and resources to places where the military outlook is more favorable and where it can regroup and grow. Even as it sees the territory under its control shrinking, it presumably is dispatching trained killers to the homelands of its enemies.

Meanwhile, IS's well-publicized activities inspire other extremist groups. In central Africa, for example, Boko Haram, which has pledged its allegiance to IS, has a more loosely organized presence that seems to rely on terror for the sake of terror. Well armed and aggressively led, Boko Haram possesses combat capabilities that exceed those of some militaries in the region. That makes Boko Haram a significant destabilizing force in an area where numerous governments – especially those that lean toward democracy – are innately fragile.

One thing that IS, Boko Haram, and other extremist groups have in common is their reprehensible treatment of women. Rape and kidnapping are standard, as are keeping and selling women as sex slaves, and, in numerous cases, executing women. This is not new; rape and other mistreatment of women have long occurred during conflict. But the persistence of such evil says something about the fundamental nature of today's terrorist organizations, and the tendency to give such matters only secondary attention says something about contemporary society. This chapter argues that this behavior should not be taken for granted or treated as a subsidiary matter. Confronting terrorism is in part a feminist issue, but the voices of women have yet to be heard in full chorus about this.

In addition to their core, on-site constituencies, groups such as Al Qaeda and IS inspire followers who are unknown to the parent organizations. The shooters in the December 2015 killings in San Bernardino, California, appeared to have received no direct orders from IS, although they had posted online their declaration of allegiance to the group. This is the kind of terrorism that is most confounding to those devising counterterrorism measures because most of these terrorists remain undetectable until after the fact.

Still to be determined is whether the IS "state" model gives an extremist organization more resilience, because of its social/political infrastructure, or makes it more vulnerable, because it offers more defined physical and financial targets. If the latter is the case, will IS and other such organizations restructure as less visible, but still deadly, "virtual" groups that maintain their structure in cyberspace and target their enemies' physical (and cyber) homelands?

This matter is complicated by the expressed desire of groups such as Al Qaeda and IS to pull their non-Muslim enemies into combat on the extremists' home turf – in countries such as Iraq and Syria – where the "infidels" can be worn down until a final apocalyptic battle takes place. But no terrorist organization can indefinitely sustain conventional combat against superior militaries such as those of the United States and its allies. So, what comes next in the evolution? Somewhere there are aspiring terrorist leaders who are studying the strengths and weaknesses of the IS caliphate and planning a successor terrorist state with more sustainable military and governmental structures. Those confronting terrorism must anticipate the next moves of extremist strategists.

Chapter 4 examines in detail the role of media in the evolution of terrorism. Osama bin Laden understood the value of publicity. Before the 2001 attacks on the United States, he occasionally granted interviews to Western journalists, knowing that this visibility would heighten his influence among his fellow jihadists. After the 9/11 attacks, he relied on video messages produced by Al Qaeda's in-house production arm, *As Sahab* (The Cloud). These messages, which appeared on Al Jazeera and other television and online venues, further established bin Laden as either "the world's number one terrorist," or "the world's number one champion of Islam," depending on who was watching. Other Al Qaeda leaders, such as Abu Musab al-Zarqawi, commander of Al Qaeda in Iraq, focused even more on media, issuing online news releases and disseminating online training videos.

Jumping ahead to IS, the sophistication of extremist media content has advanced significantly, incorporating well-produced "documentaries" about the IS cause and patient one-on-one recruiting on social media. In addition to its usefulness in recruiting, this media expertise gets to the heart of the "homegrown" terrorist phenomenon. Those extremists do not develop in isolation; they are courted from afar through skillfully designed messaging, and they pass along this content to others. The resulting networks significantly enhance the capabilities of extremist groups.

The response to the products of terrorists' media savvy has been – to put it charitably – inadequate. From the earliest days after the 9/11 attacks, the US and other governments have found it difficult to identify their audiences and refine their media messaging.

This is enormously important, because IS, Al Qaeda, and other extremist groups rely on media-based recruitment to increase their personnel faster than their opponents can kill them or entice them to desert. This underscores the need for a more assertive and better planned media strategy that can disrupt that recruitment process and shrink terrorist ranks.

In Chapter 5, we consider what might lie ahead. It is not a pleasant picture. In addition to political strategies, countering IS and other terror groups must include a firm kinetic response. Examples drawn from conflicts such as the Vietnam and Iraq Wars are instructive about counterinsurgency and asymmetric warfare, with important lessons about avoiding overreliance on airpower and other traditional tactics. On one level, the debate about military responses to terrorism comes down to the question of what price those leading these efforts are willing to pay. Would, for example, the American public support yet another deployment of a large ground force into the Middle East, with the human and financial costs that this would entail? The prospect of going back into Iraq or elsewhere in the region has negligible appeal, but that might change if there were new 9/11-type (or worse) attacks on the US homeland.

Dealing with IS, Boko Haram, Al Shabaab, and other groups requires military strategies geared to indigenous capabilities. But in countries where the armed forces have been unable to effectively fight extremist groups, what course of action should more powerful nations follow? Provide military aid? Send in trainers? Rely on small numbers of Special Forces to assist local troops? Supply more robust assistance, deploying many "boots on the ground"?

If this were a matter of Russian troops marching into Estonia, the decision process would be straightforward: honor the North Atlantic Treaty Organization (NATO) commitment to Estonia, or not. But most terrorist groups have not, so far, been regarded as existential threats or as state-level adversaries covered by treaty provisions, and so commitment to strong measures has been sporadic. Further, coalitions have proved flimsy, as can be seen in the reluctance of many Arab states to participate fully in the fight against IS, a fight that includes a dimension of Sunni–Shia conflict that, like a powerful magnet, has drawn in regional non-Arab powers such as Iran and Turkey. Alliances need to be formalized in terms of antiterrorism purposes, and their members' responsibilities must be made clear and accepted. Without such steps, those engaged in fighting against terrorists on the battlefield will find their efforts frustrating and unending. Just as NATO was created to counter the post–World War II Soviet threat, a new alliance should be formed against terrorist states.

Even with more effective battlefield efforts to deal with IS, Boko Haram, and their kin, the roots of extremism will still exist and will be likely to produce another generation of violence. Ensuring that these roots wither out requires finding ways to end the political and cultural estrangement of the men and women – most of them young – who have proved susceptible to extremist organizations' appeal. This involves having a public diplomacy strategy at least as sophisticated as the military one. Educational exchanges, workshops for budding entrepreneurs that can help generate jobs, more careful listening to voices from countries and communities where extremism has appeal ... such incremental steps would capitalize on "soft power," which relies on attraction rather than coercion. These measures might open doors to hopefulness that undercuts feelings of marginalization and the allure of violence.

Given that the level of terroristic violence requires immediate and forceful response, counting on soft power may seem a wishy-washy distraction. But if we are not to endure terrorism indefinitely, we must adopt a diverse array of tactics that can have long-term effect. A significant population of young people could turn their lives in alternate directions, either heeding the call of extremists or rejecting that call and pursuing constructive futures. If they are to follow the latter path, they will need encouragement and tangible help.

Mourning victims. Launching air strikes. Recoiling from Islam and those who practice it. So far, the response to terrorism has amounted to little more than ad hoc and poorly conceived measures. That reactive approach won't work.

Needed instead is a systemic adjustment of political and military priorities. For those in the West, dealing with IS should lead to a reappraisal of the overall relationship with the Arab world, with emphasis on pushing Arab nations to take more responsibility for policing their own neighborhood. Failure to do so and instead committing to greater Western military involvement would gratify terrorist leaders. The presence of non-Muslims on Muslim land is a powerful recruiting tool. More widely, long-term counterterrorism assistance to countries such as Nigeria and Indonesia should be upgraded to meet their specific needs. Governments that are willing to address terrorism in constructive ways – meaning not ignoring basic human rights – must be helped in protecting their own countries.

All these are just pieces of a solution that is unlikely to be effective unless derived from a comprehensive reappraisal of the causes of terrorism and ways to remedy them. That is a complex task, and the public needs to understand all that will be involved. At least initially, terrorist acts are likely to increase in number and ferocity as extremists find themselves with their backs against a wall, as has become the case with IS in Iraq and Syria. The responses, military and political, will be costly in money and lives, and will require cutbacks in meeting other pressing needs. Most important will be sustaining public resolve to deal with this problem in ways that do not undercut fundamental values. If fear and anger come to dominate how we live, the extremists will have won, regardless of how severely they are punished on the battlefield.

This book is designed to provide a broad outline of issues related to modern terrorism, with emphasis on how terrorism continues to evolve. As of this writing, IS is under siege and taking heavy losses in its principal strongholds in Iraq and Syria. Concerted military pressure apparently is prevailing, although many IS fighters presumably have escaped to fight another day and in other ways. And while much of the world's attention is focused on Iraq and Syria, terrorism's roots grow deeper elsewhere in the world.

Consider how far terrorism has come from the days of the individual assassin or bomb thrower, the hostage-takers of the 1980s, and even from the rise of Al Qaeda two decades ago. IS seized and held Iraq's second largest city and other territory for three years. It created a system of governance that provided basic services and supervised an oil-based economy. The "caliphate" (despite its pretensions, a terrorist rather than religious entity) became a physical reality, at least for a while.

What happens now, not just with IS but with whatever the next manifestations of terrorist organizations? Where will the continuing maturation of violent extremism take us? Better understanding the evolutionary path of terrorism may help us anticipate what lies ahead.

Another purpose of this book is to illustrate the connections among the central elements of today's terrorism, including political violence, weaponized religion, and astute use of new media. These factors do not exist in isolation; they act upon and with one another. Also, they exist not solely within the realm of the terrorist. For instance, parallels with terrorists' media acumen can be seen in Russia's use of media to foment political unrest.

Part of comprehending a more holistic view of terrorism involves understanding the appeal of violence – how it is fostered by political and economic weakness in numerous societies and how it can be exacerbated by malicious interpretations of religious doctrine. "Holy war" has plagued civilization for many centuries, and religion's role in today's terrorism must be addressed directly. That should be accompanied, however, with the recognition that religion is often used by perpetrators of violence merely in attempting to disguise their bloody and, at root, irreligious criminality.

When the twenty-first century began, few people expected that it would become a "terrorism era" likely to last for decades. That, however, is a harsh reality we must recognize. Terrorism will never vanish, but the damage it causes can be reduced. Responding effectively to causes of terrorism and to terroristic acts will require a broad and sophisticated understanding of what we are dealing with.

I hope this book will help.

1   The Nature of the Beast

During the Cold War, we understood the menace of ballistic missiles carrying nuclear warheads, and we were fairly certain where they would come from. This allowed us to construct relatively orderly military and psychological defenses against this danger. There were close calls, but the dreaded nuclear exchange and resulting annihilation of millions never happened.

The acts of terrorism that have occurred during the first years of the twenty-first century are smaller in scale, but disproportionately frightening. Instead of missiles raining down upon us, we might face one person detonating a suicide vest in the middle of a crowded downtown or driving a truck through a group of celebrating tourists. Instead of millions dying in a single attack, the casualties so far have ranged from a handful to several thousand (although terrorists might potentially use weapons of mass destruction, WMD). Nevertheless, the violence perpetrated by terrorists produces fear because its causes and remedies are so difficult to grasp. Why would someone do this? Who is responsible? How can we stop it?

When the United States and Soviet Union neared the brink of nuclear catastrophe, there was hope that the two nations' leaders would save the day through direct diplomacy ... and they did. Terrorism is more amorphous.

Negotiate? With whom?

Remove a terrorist leader, such as Osama bin Laden? Beyond symbolic revenge, what does it accomplish?

Go to war, in the traditional sense? Where and against whom?

The lack of reassuring answers to such questions underscores terrorism's ability to produce fear and confusion as well as inflict casualties. That is why terrorism casts such a pervasive shadow. The most powerful weapon of terrorism is terror.

WHAT IS TERRORISM?

Search a library or the Internet for a definition of *terrorism* and you might be overwhelmed by the results. Nations, jurists, and scholars offer dozens of contemporary definitions, and if you prefer a more historical approach you can see how ancient Romans, French revolutionaries, and the League of Nations used the term. As terrorism has evolved, so have the definitions, ranging from those of the 1970s that were driven by a spate of airplane hijackings, to more recent ones that focus on mass casualties produced by vicious political "statements." The spate of IS attacks in Europe in 2015–16 are examples of this.

Lawyers being lawyers, some of the definitions are unwieldy, and governments being governments, different agencies within the same nation may use different definitions. I prefer one of the shortest I found, which is the US Code provision related to the Department of State's annual country reports about terrorism:

> "[T]errorism" means premeditated, politically motivated violence perpetrated against noncombatant targets by subnational groups or clandestine agents.

Brief as that is, it can still be parsed, but the heart of its meaning is *politically motivated violence directed at civilians.* Unstated in the statute is an important corollary: *designed to create terror within a general population* to reach the goal, however remote, of compelling a government to change policy, which might range from a prisoner release to withdrawal from certain territory. Like most definitions, this one has a share of fuzziness, such as the reference to "clandestine agents." "Agency" may imply a direct connection, as when orders are issued and followed. This is not always the case. Numerous terrorist attacks have been carried out by people *inspired*, not *directed*, by IS or other groups. Yet another distinction with the scope of terrorism relates to "domestic" and "lone-wolf" terrorists, described later in this chapter.

Defining *terrorism* with as much precision as is possible is important because if the legal system is to be a bulwark against terrorism through prosecution of accused terrorists, juries are likely to want a clear definition that tightly fits such acts, especially because defendants may face long prison terms or even death penalty. Further, as will be discussed later in the book, legal definitions related to terrorism are also important because if they are overbroad governments might use that breadth to intrude on their citizens' privacy, infringe on free speech, and otherwise limit civil liberties.

In addition to definitional matters, politics may shape perceptions of terrorism, which can lead to a standard based on "it depends on the eye of the beholder." Was, for example, Menachem Begin, prime minister of Israel from 1977 to 1983 and a co-winner (with Egypt's president Anwar al-Sadat) of the 1978 Nobel Peace Prize, a terrorist or a "freedom fighter" when in 1946, as leader of the Irgun, a Zionist underground group, he ordered the bombing of the King David Hotel in Jerusalem in which 91 people were killed?

Some might believe that the quest for a Jewish state justified this kind of action. It was directed against the British, whose Mandate for Palestine administrative offices were in the hotel. Others would argue that the end does *not* necessarily justify the means, particularly in a case such as the King David Hotel attack in which most of those killed were not British troops but clerical staff and non-British hotel workers. The attack would seem to conform to the definition of terrorism cited earlier in this chapter.

Terrorism comprises numerous variations on a theme of physical and psychological violence. Rarely is it mindless; terrorists seek to legitimize their destructiveness by wrapping it in political or religious purpose. Osama bin Laden, shortly after the 2001 attacks on the United States, stated that "neither America, nor anyone living there, will ever enjoy safety until we can first see it as a reality in Palestine and before all the infidel armies quit the land of

Muhammad."[1] As political issues, recognizing Palestinians' rights and removing Western troops from Muslim countries are worthy of debate, but making the leap to terroristic violence as a calculated tactic moves into another realm altogether.

This is the essence of terrorism: trying to achieve a previously unobtainable political outcome or avenge a perceived political crime by abandoning conventional processes and instead embracing violence directed at a general population. Whether it was Osama bin Laden attacking the United States, Timothy McVeigh blowing up the Federal Building in Oklahoma City, or the Tsarnaev brothers bombing the Boston Marathon, their actions – regardless of the reasons behind them – transcended "politics" and violated norms of civilized society.

During the past two decades, terrorism has become a part of life in much of the world. Despite its intruding into the public's consciousness, its causes and motivations are little understood, and responses to it remain more emotional than strategic. Trying to counter violence with wildly aimed hatred is futile at best and likely to prove counterproductive. News coverage of terrorism-related topics is often unhelpful. It tends to be superficial, focusing on events of the moment without providing context. Entertainment media also shape public perceptions of terror. Film and television provide stirring, but often misleading, depictions of terrorists and how to respond to terrorism. All this is reactive, but to have any chance of success, combating the extremism that leads to violence must be *proactive*.

Few governments are good at this. They find it politically expedient to thrash about noisily, spending heavily on programs of questionable efficacy. Government officials and their allies in the private sector know a gold mine when they see one, and so for more than a decade they have been able to manipulate budget makers' reluctance to deny funding requests for programs and hardware that are attractively

---

[1] "Osama bin Laden's Oath to America," in Raymond Ibrahim (ed.), *The Al Qaeda Reader* (New York: Broadway Books, 2007), 195.

wrapped in the rhetoric of counterterrorism. Even small-town American police forces have successfully applied for federal funding for tanklike vehicles to protect the local pumpkin festival.[2]

SEMANTICS AND STRATEGIES

After the 2001 attacks in the United States, the fashionable term for this was waging a "war on terror." As rhetoric, this had its uses, but it also had its limits. Declaring war on a definable enemy, such as "war on Al Qaeda," is easy to grasp, but how does one wage war on a concept, such as "terror"? Who or what precisely is the enemy? How does a nation go about fighting such a war?

Such questions (as well as the association of "war on terror" with the George W. Bush presidency) led to a rechristening during Barack Obama's administration. The "war on terror" gave way to countering violent extremism (CVE) as a preventive approach, while kinetic measures, such as law enforcement responses and military action, were labeled "counterterrorism." CVE is a bit clunky and does not stir the blood in the way "war" does, but it connotes a broader approach that emphasizes nonviolent measures. Still unclear, however, is what constitutes "violent extremism." It sounds unpleasant, but as a legal and practical matter, how is it to be "countered"?

As policy makers (and, to a lesser extent, the public) have realized that addressing terrorism requires more than punch and counterpunch, intervening in and disrupting radicalization has become more credible. US Under Secretary of State, Sarah Sewall, defined CVE as a "comprehensive, preventive, and civilian-centered approach" designed to prevent people "from taking up violent extremism in the first place."[3]

That goal makes sense, but differentiating CVE and "counterterrorism" may be a false distinction. It makes more sense to view

---

[2] https://publicintelligence.net/coburn-uasi-waste-report/ [accessed July 1, 2016].
[3] Sarah Sewall, "Countering Violent Extremism: How Human Rights and Good Governance Help Prevent Terrorism," February 29, 2016, www.state.gov/j/remarks/253870.htm [accessed May 3, 2016].

them jointly as part of a continuum. (And by late 2016, some terrorism experts at the US State Department were saying that the term *CVE* had fallen into disfavor and *counterterrorism* in its broad sense was in vogue.)

Whatever the terminology, pathways toward violence must be blocked, and policy makers should understand that a mixed approach to terrorism is essential in doing so. In dealing with IS, for instance, a solely military approach will not work because IS tacticians are smart enough to disperse their personnel. In addition to battlefield efforts, reducing IS recruiting capabilities is essential and must be linked to any military strategy. Designing and communicating messages for diverse audiences about why *not* to join an extremist group and how to achieve political goals through other means is a good way to weaken IS and its ilk. Combating terrorism is done largely through attrition, and this requires that the terrorist organizations' recruiting faucet be turned off.

Identifying the appropriate audience and developing the appropriate messaging in such an approach are crucial tasks in undermining terrorists' appeal. Many players are involved in this. The news media are part of the process because news depictions do much to develop the context in which violent extremism is justified by some and opposed by others. Feelings about injustice, real and imagined, that spread through parts of the Muslim world (including the Arab diaspora) contribute to the alienation in which extremist sentiment can take root. News coverage of conflicts in the Middle East during which Western and other militaries inflict civilian casualties can fuel a desire to respond, especially when the violence is presented without adequate explanation of its causes and complexities.

Since the advent of satellite television channels and online news providers, information is both more accessible and more varied. The information battleground is hotly contested. In the Arab world, television channels such as Saudi-backed Al Arabiya and Hizbollah's Al Manar offer their audiences very different worldviews and versions of events. Online venues range from those created by IS to sites managed by the US State Department. The result is a cacophony of messages and a competition for credibility and attention.

In a news environment in which so much emphasis is placed on speed and sensational framing, reporting that provides context may be in short supply. Explaining terrorism is not justifying terrorism, but it is easy for news organizations to be swept up in the emotional reaction to a terror attack or to be wary of trying to sail against the current of angry public opinion. Rare are the exceptions. Shortly after the 9/11 attacks in 2001, *The New Yorker* published commentary by Susan Sontag in which she criticized news coverage, writing that those "licensed to follow the event seem to have joined together in a campaign to infantilize the public. Where is the acknowledgement that this was not a 'cowardly' attack on 'civilization' or 'liberty' or 'humanity' or 'the free world,' but an attack on the world's self-proclaimed superpower, undertaken as a consequence of specific American alliances and actions?"[4]

Such viewpoints tend to be disparaged and marginalized. Few mainstream news organizations are confident enough to publish this kind of material. The news media are sensitive to the opinions of their audience and their advertisers, especially when emotion driven, and so are likely to avoid contrarian probing. That is good for business, if not for journalism. As terrorism becomes recognized as more than just a transient phenomenon, honest debate about its causes will be essential in devising appropriate responses.

Furthermore, introspection – however painful it might be – is essential if policy makers are to understand what drives terrorism. Martha Crenshaw wrote in 2016: "I often think that our current counterterrorism focus on 'countering the narrative' neglects to consider how our actions affirm and reinforce the jihadist narrative. Perhaps I am too critical here, but it seems to me that American leaders and opinion makers in particular think of their/the enemy's 'narrative' as entirely self-generated. We see that it is emotionally powerful, but

---

[4] Susan Sontag, "First Reactions," *The New Yorker*, September 24, 2001, 42.

we don't see why. This problem is related to a tendency to spotlight the means of transmission of propaganda ... rather than the content of the message."[5]

Related to this is the politically comfortable notion that a "war on terrorism" can be "won." Certainly, military punishment can be inflicted on terrorist groups, as was the case with Al Qaeda in Afghanistan in 2001 and IS in Iraq in 2016. In these and similar instances, the terrorist organizations may have been severely wounded, but they weren't killed. As Brian Michael Jenkins observed: "War, in modern American military tradition, implies a finite undertaking – a clear beginning and end, while 'combatting terrorism' implies an enduring task. In war, we seek victory. In combatting crime, we have no expectation of an ultimate police victory over all criminals and the end of crime. Instead, we expect the authorities to keep crime under control – that is, within limits society can tolerate ... We can weaken terrorist groups, create a hostile environment for them, and take other measures to mitigate the threat, but can we realistically expect to achieve a final victory over terrorism?"[6]

In 2016, *The Economist* described an "age of humdrum terror" in which random terrorist attacks are "fiendishly hard to prevent" partly because "neither great planning nor great intelligence is required to carry out such attacks." Nevertheless, the risk to individual citizens is minimal; between 2003 and 2013, the chance of an American being killed in a terrorist attack was one in 56 million (while the chance of that same American being the victim of a non-terrorist homicide was one in 20,000). Terrorists' success is mostly psychological, enhanced, according to *The Economist*, by "politicians who glibly talk of threats being 'existential.' "[7]

[5] Martha Crenshaw, Brian Michael Jenkins, and Bruce Hoffman, "How Much Really Changed About Terrorism on 9/11?," *Defense One*, September 12, 2016, www .defenseone.com/ideas/2016/09/how-much-really-changed-about-terrorism-911/ 131438/print [accessed November 1, 2016].

[6] Crenshaw, Jenkins, and Hoffman, "How Much Really Changed?"

[7] "Learning to Live with It," *Economist*, September 3, 2016, 53–4.

Even if the threat it poses is sometimes overblown, that is little consolation to the families of its victims. Terrorism remains a blight on civil society that must be assertively countered, regardless of whether it can be eradicated. Much of that effort must be devoted to limiting the growth of the number of self-styled jihadists. Whether through social media or other methods, the relatively large-scale recruitment and long-distance training of extremists in scattered places poses new challenges for counterterrorism. During the 1990s, when Al Qaeda was building its strength, its recruiting took place in a more tightly controlled way and the numbers it sought for its operations were far smaller than those that IS needed when it seized significant amounts of territory. Understanding recruitment and countering it require a thorough understanding of who the players are.

GLOBALIZED TERRORISM

Beginning in 1997, the US State Department has maintained a list of "designated foreign terrorist organizations." By early 2017, the list included dozens of groups, some well-known ones such as Hamas and Boko Haram, and others of lesser notoriety, such as the Indonesian organization Jemaah Anshorut Tauhid. Once a group is added to the list, its members may not legally enter the United States, any financial assets it has within the United States are frozen, and it becomes illegal for American citizens to provide support of any kind – money, housing, training, and more – to any member of the group.[8] The State Department also maintains a list of individuals who are similarly restricted. (The Treasury Department maintains a longer list that includes individuals and entities restricted as a result of US international sanctions.)

Other governments have similar lists; the British Home Office's roster of "Proscribed Terrorist Organizations" is a good example.[9] It describes forbidden activities and states that it is a criminal offence

[8] www.state.gov/j/ct/rls/other/des/123085.htm [accessed February 20, 2017].
[9] www.gov.uk/government/uploads/system/uploads/attachment_data/file/472956/Proscription-update-20151030.pdf [accessed January 30, 2016].

to "wear clothing or carry or display articles in public in such a way or in such circumstances as arouse reasonable suspicion that an individual is a member or supporter of the proscribed organization." (The roster includes a separate list of fourteen groups "linked to Northern Ireland–related terrorism.")

Such inventories are worth examining because they illustrate the breadth of terrorism. Until reminded of this by these lists or individual incidents, many tend to associate terrorism exclusively with the Middle East. But countries such as India, Indonesia, Somalia, Uzbekistan, and others are home to terrorist groups found on the US and British lists.

Terrorism as a global phenomenon is not new, but the connected nature of many terrorist groups and the virtual linkage between terrorist centers and individuals marks a dangerous maturation of violent extremism. Al Qaeda took steps toward the "franchise" design with its offspring in the Islamic Maghreb, in the Arabian Peninsula, in the Indian Subcontinent, and others. This geographic diversification, which occurred gradually during the decade after the 9/11 attacks, made the killing of Osama bin Laden in 2011 more a symbolic victory than a substantive blow to Al Qaeda. By the time of the raid by US special operators on bin Laden's hideout in Abbottabad, Pakistan, Al Qaeda's structure had evolved from classic hierarchy to a loose, flexible network.

IS has followed a different path. It has maintained centralized control, with its leader Abu Bakr al-Baghdadi based (presumably) in Iraq and Syria as of early 2016. But while this IS homeland was being subjected to military attacks by the United States and others, the organization was establishing itself in Libya (a move that constituted an incipient threat to other North African countries), winning pledges of affiliation from the likes of Boko Haram in Nigeria, and inspiring attacks as far away as Indonesia. Further, IS continued to bring formalized structure to areas where it operated, designating places where it had established a presence, such as Sinai, as "provinces" (*wilayas*) of its "caliphate." Closer to home, al-Baghdadi reportedly had devolved command authority to numerous lieutenants, thus ensuring the continuation of IS if he was killed.

Al Qaeda is certainly still with us, but it as of mid-2016 was receiving far less public attention due to the ongoing battlefield and terrorist operations of IS. Al Qaeda's expansion into South Asia was its first significant foray beyond Southwest Asia, the Middle East, and North Africa, and it poses a particular potential threat because of tensions between India and Pakistan and the region's Hindu and Muslim populations.

IS moved forcefully into Afghanistan, where it contests the Taliban for radical leadership in that country, and where it might come into direct confrontation with US ground forces. The growing strength of IS within Afghanistan was a factor in the Obama administration's decision to slow the withdrawal of American troops from there and to expand the mission of those troops to include anti-IS, as well as anti-Taliban, targeting.[10]

Meanwhile, IS's Nigeria-based affiliate, Boko Haram, extended its activity into Niger, Cameroon, and Chad, and began referring to the region as the "Province of West Africa" of the IS caliphate. In Niger, Boko Haram has found success in recruiting young men while driving away those who do not sympathize with their movement.[11] Other than generating spurts of notoriety, such as in 2014 when it kidnapped more than 200 schoolgirls, Boko Haram receives relatively little attention outside its region, despite having killed more than 17,000 and displaced more than a million. Nigerian journalist Tolu Ogunlesi observed, "In Nigeria, we expect most terrorist attacks to go unnoticed by the world."[12]

But terrorist groups in this part of Africa, reported Carlotta Gall, are deepening their collaboration, "using modern communications

---

[10] Gordon Lubold, "U.S. Clears Path to Target Islamic State in Afghanistan," *Wall Street Journal*, January 19, 2016.

[11] Yaroslav Trofimov, "Expanding beyond Nigeria, Boko Haram Threatens Region," *Wall Street Journal*, December 3, 2015.

[12] Tolu Ogunlesi, "Terror's Nameless Victims in Nigeria," *New York Times*, December 2, 2015.

and a sophisticated system of roving trainers to share military tactics, media strategies, and ways of transferring money." This is evidenced, added Gall, by the spread of suicide bombings and use of improvised explosive devices. Local actors have expanded their reach, becoming pan-national threats. France and the United States have sent troops (totaling around 4,000) to help strengthen several African countries' defenses against these groups.[13]

In Southeast Asia, especially in Indonesia and Malaysia, the globalization of terrorism is also apparent. In addition to wholly local groups, IS is believed to be exerting long-distance influence. Indonesian authorities traced a bombing in Jakarta in January 2016 to the head of a Southeast Asian unit fighting as part of IS in Syria and Iraq. A major local terrorist group, Jemaah Islamiya, which was responsible for a 2002 bombing in Bali that killed more than 200 persons, had seen its capabilities degraded by fierce antiterrorist efforts, and IS has partially filled this vacuum. Significant levels of support for IS have been found in the region.[14]

Wherever they operate, IS and its allies are skilled at taking advantage of local conditions: lack of jobs, pervasive corruption, unresponsive government, and other factors that make it easier to recruit people for extremist activities. Draping political and economic matters in religious righteousness heightens the IS appeal. With its African connections and its recruitment in parts of East Asia, IS clearly is a global threat. Considering the difficulties the United States had in dealing with Al Qaeda (including finding bin Laden) in a relatively localized mission, the growing reach of IS will require expanded and innovative countermeasures.

Although IS's dramatic behavior, such as conducting public executions, attracted much of the media's attention, other terrorist groups – including Al Qaeda – were more quietly going about their business. A report by an array of terrorism experts, published in late

---

[13] Carlotta Gall, "Jihadists Deepen Collaboration in North Africa," *New York Times*, January 1, 2016.

[14] "After Jakarta," *Economist*, January 23, 2016, 32–4.

2016, noted the "local-first" approach that has been embraced by Al Qaeda and smaller groups. This involves building a bottom-up organization with its foundation grounded in local militias' jihadist efforts. According to the report, "Al Qaeda's strategy is more gradualist. It believes that Muslims must be educated first on sharia, that the idea of jihad must be popularized, and that Muslims must be convinced to take up arms as the only method of emancipation." That said, the report also notes that Al Qaeda and IS have much in common: "They are both exploiting disenfranchised or disillusioned Sunni youth in the Middle East and abroad. They are both undermining the existing state system and contributing to expanding wars in the region. They are both normalizing the belief that violent jihad is necessary in order to defend the Sunni community globally."[15]

Al Qaeda's evolution is evident in the activity of Al Qaeda in the Arabian Peninsula (AQAP) during the civil war in Yemen. Michael Horton wrote that AQAP has benefited from this conflict because, like other such groups, it "thrives in environments where state authority is weak or non-existent, where poverty is endemic, and where opposition forces are fragmented." Horton also observed that AQAP, "which is now better funded and armed than at any point in its history" implemented a three-part strategy: First, it "realized that it cannot alienate those it seeks to govern by enforcing all aspects of its understanding of Islamic law," and instead is "demonstrating its capacity to 'govern' and provide basic services, most particularly security." Second, it strengthened its ties with "Yemen's tribes whose power had been enhanced by the civil war." And third, AQAP enmeshed itself within local fighting groups. Further, noted Horton, "AQAP's prioritization of the formation of more intelligence cells aligns with its leadership's embrace of what could be called the long war. It is employing tactics that will prevent it from being

---

[15] *The Jihadi Threat: ISIS, Al Qaeda, and Beyond*, United States Institute of Peace, December 2016, 6–8, www.usip.org/sites/default/files/The-Jihadi-Threat-ISIS-Al-Qaeda-and-Beyond.pdf [accessed February 10, 2017].

easily targeted and that allow it to continue to act through proxies." Overall, wrote Horton, AQAP's "ideological and religious goals have been made secondary – at least temporarily – to its goal of securing local support."[16]

This ability to adapt underscores the fact that the weed of terrorism not only must be chopped off at the surface, but also pulled out by its roots, which apparently are growing longer and stronger.

COUNTERTERRORISM TAKES SHAPE

President George W. Bush, in a speech to a joint session of Congress on September 20, 2001, said, "Our war on terror begins with al Qaeda, but it does not end there. It will not end until every terrorist group of global reach has been found, stopped and defeated."[17] Taken literally, that promised a war unlikely to ever end. In his memoir, Bush justified his use of "war" rather than treating terrorism as a matter for law enforcement: "Suicidal men willing to fly passenger planes into buildings were not common criminals. They could not be deterred by the threat of prosecution. They had declared war on America. To protect the country, we had to wage war against the terrorists."[18]

In 2013, Bush's successor, Barack Obama, set aside the "war on terror" terminology. "Beyond Afghanistan," he said, "we must define our effort not as a boundless 'global war on terror' – but rather as a series of persistent, targeted efforts to dismantle specific networks of violent extremists that threaten America. In many cases, this will involve partnerships with other countries." He added, "The next

---

[16] Michael Horton, "Fighting the Long War: The Evolution of Al-Qa'ida in the Arabian Peninsula," *CTC Sentinel* 9 (1120), January 23, 2017, www.ctc.usma.edu/posts/fighting-the-long-war-the-evolution-of-al-qaida-in-the-arabian-peninsula [accessed February 8, 2017].

[17] George W. Bush, "Address to the Joint Session of the 107th Congress," September 20, 2011, http://georgewbush-whitehouse.archives.gov/infocus/bushrecord/documents/Selected_Speeches_George_W_Bush.pdf, 68 [accessed October 20, 2016].

[18] George W. Bush, *Decision Points* (New York: Broadway Books, 2010), 154.

element of our strategy involves addressing the underlying grievances and conflicts that feed extremism."[19] Obama's approach was an expansion of policy beyond the military-first emphasis of the Bush administration. By no means was Obama abandoning force; he defended his use of drones to target terrorists and made clear that conventional and special operations warfare against groups such as Al Qaeda would continue. But he also talked about supporting political and economic development in countries where extremism could take root.

This is the essence of a broad approach to counterterrorism. It is a complex mechanism with many moving parts, and may be more difficult to intellectually grasp than a straightforward reliance on hard power. Even the economics of such an effort are complicated; foreign aid programs must be supported as more than just doing good, but also as essential elements in undermining extremism.

Obama also cited a commitment to building democratic institutions, which has long been a central tenet of US foreign policy. Although this may sound good to Americans and others who live in today's democracies, its allure may be considerably less in countries where the citizens yearn for stability and safety more than anything else, and care little about what political system provides them. In the minds of many, "democracy" has become tainted, and promoting it is seen as guise for a presence by the West in areas where it does not belong.

The principles of counterterrorism outlined by Obama made sense, but then they were processed in the bureaucratic machinery of the US government, several other countries, and the United Nations. Some of the players gravitated to counterterrorism because they genuinely desired to be helpful, but others did so because they knew that plenty of money would be available for programs that could nurture their own mini-bureaucracies.

---

[19] www.whitehouse.gov/the-press-office/2013/05/23/remarks-president-barack-obama [accessed June 12, 2016].

As part of this process, there had to be meetings – many meetings, some of which were even dubbed "summits." The White House Summit on Countering Violent Extremism in February 2015 focused on "community-oriented approaches to counter hateful extremist ideologies that radicalize, recruit, or incite to violence." At this meeting, *CVE* was defined as encompassing "the preventative aspects of counterterrorism as well as interventions to undermine the attraction of extremist movements and ideologies." The tools for doing so were to be social media, religious leaders, civil society, and youth engagement.[20] Interestingly, the summit's overview statement did not mention actions that might be taken in prisons, which are often incubators for radicalization, or the importance of jobs for the young people whose idleness makes them easier prey for extremist recruiters.

The US approach was better distilled in comments by Under Secretary of State, Sewall, who stated that "CVE seeks to move U.S. counterterrorism toward a more proactive, affirmative, and preventive approach. By containing the spread of terrorist threats, CVE is an essential complement to military efforts, from drone strikes in Libya to the global campaign against ISIL." She also cited a study that found that "over the last 25 years, up to 92 percent of all terrorist attacks have occurred in countries where state-sponsored violence – like torture and extra-judicial killings – was widespread."[21]

Several of the countries Sewall referred to are "friends" of the United States, and more will be required from them than platitudes about their commitment to CVE. Fundamental changes in how they govern will be essential, but US policy has always stopped short of pushing hard for such reforms, and the countries in question prefer to assert their sovereignty by ignoring even gentle pressure from allies.

[20] "Fact Sheet: The White House Summit on Countering Violent Extremism," February 18, 2015, www.whitehouse.gov/the-press-office/2015/02/18/fact-sheet-white-house-summit-countering-violent-extremism [accessed January 26, 2016].
[21] www.state.gov/j/remarks/249839.htm [accessed November 1, 2016].

Rami Khouri took this argument further, citing "the causal influence of Western policies in this grim cycle of global violence." Specifically, wrote Khouri:

> The countering violent extremism approach ignores four of the most important drivers of political violence and terrorism in the Middle East: 1) sustained socioeconomic stress, deprivation and marginalization, including rampant official corruption, that leave several hundred million people destitute and powerless; 2) chronic, Western-supported authoritarianism and dictatorships that leave citizens without any political rights in most of the societies that generate terrorism; 3) the impact of sustained Western militarism in the region over the last few decades, especially the Anglo-American war in Iraq; and 4) the persistent radicalizing impact for the past half-century of the Arab-Israeli conflict, Israeli colonization of Arab lands and U.S.-led Western acquiescence in Israeli policies.[22]

In addition to acknowledging Khouri's points, as the policies related to countering violent extremism develop further, challenging questions should be asked about the presumption that a Western model of political life is suitable throughout the world. This matters because if those who want to counter extremism offer alternatives that lack appeal to contested audiences, the outcome will be predictably negative. And, as we will see, the political masterminds behind IS and its kin are well attuned to the aspirations of these audiences and are skilled at taking advantage of their dissatisfaction.

TERRORISM'S DYNAMISM

Terrorism evolves to keep pace with the political and technological environments in which it exists. Just a few decades ago, terrorism

---

[22] Rami G. Khouri, "Beware the Hoax of Countering Violent Extremism," Al Jazeera America, September 29, 2015, http://america.aljazeera.com/opinions/2015/9/beware-the-hoax-of-countering-violent-extremism.html [accessed October 1, 2015].

"spectaculars" consisted primarily of hijacking airplanes and then relying on news coverage to convey the terrorists' demands and political views to the public. Terrorists would sometimes hold press briefings to make certain their messages were delivered, and they capitalized on the appetite of news organizations (especially television) to cover sensational events.

By the 1990s, terrorism had grown far nastier. Instead of exchanging hijacked air passengers for imprisoned fellow extremists, terrorists inflicted large numbers of civilian casualties through bombings. This was when Al Qaeda made its presence felt, first with a 1993 truck bomb attack on New York's World Trade Center, which killed six persons and injured more than a thousand, and then, in 1998, with attacks on the US embassies in Dar es Salaam, Tanzania and Nairobi, Kenya. These two, nearly simultaneous bombings killed 224 persons and wounded more than 4,000. In 2000, the US Navy destroyer *Cole* was attacked while refueling in Aden, Yemen, killing seventeen American sailors and wounding thirty-nine others.

Writing about the 1993 New York attack, Lawrence Wright observed that such bombings were designed in part for their symbolic value. "Theater is always a feature of terror," wrote Wright, "and these were terrorists whose dramatic ambition was unrivaled ... [and] they courted retaliation as a prod to other Muslims."[23] The terrorists were picking a fight and they relished the perverse admiration this generated among those who saw the United States as an overbearing hegemon.

By the time of the 9/11 attacks in 2001, the Madrid bombing of 2004, and the London attacks in 2005, terrorism had become more than a string of unrelated incidents. Instead, a pattern of menace had emerged, and governments began to realize that case-by-case responses would be inadequate. Just as the West had developed systemic methods for dealing with the Soviet nuclear threat during

---

[23] Lawrence Wright, *The Looming Tower: Al-Qaeda and the Road to 9/11* (New York: Knopf, 2006), 179.

the Cold War, there now was recognition that terrorism required a coherent ongoing response.

This first required determining who the enemy was. After 9/11, the answer was initially straightforward: Al Qaeda and its Taliban hosts in Afghanistan. The United States and its Afghan allies attacked, degrading and driving to cover (at least temporarily) the enemy. But then the antiterrorism strategy went woefully askew as the United States began a war in Iraq that has metastasized like a particularly virulent cancer. Elsewhere in the world, terrorist groups began to strike more viciously, and governments sought effective ways to deal with them.

Meanwhile, publics around the world became increasingly fearful as terrorists struck close to home. Beslan, Paris, Beirut, San Bernardino, Jakarta, Bamako ... the list is long and continues to grow. If a basic responsibility of a government is to protect its citizens, why have terrorists been able to strike in so many places, apparently at will?

For policy makers seeking an answer to that question, a drastic change in thinking is necessary. During the Cold War's US–Soviet Union standoff, the threat of massive nuclear retaliation – "mutually assured destruction" (MAD) – helped to deter rash acts. More recently, technology has provided new protections, such as Israel's "Iron Dome" air defense system that can intercept incoming rockets and artillery shells. Such advances are fine in defending against conventional military aggression, but are irrelevant in thwarting terrorist attacks plotted by groups without an identifiable home that can be targeted and rely on attackers who surreptitiously arrive at the site where they will unleash their violence.

In this regard, IS has changed the nature of terrorism because unlike many other terrorist organizations it has committed itself to seizing and holding territory. The United States, the United Kingdom, France, Russia, and other IS foes have thus been able to use their sophisticated air power against the IS domain. But aside from inflicting significant damage on IS forces (although apparently not sufficient to cripple IS), as well as civilian casualties in IS-controlled areas, the air attacks have produced little evidence that they are significantly impairing IS-inspired operations that take place far away. It is likely that when global news media report about IS battlefield setbacks, the IS leadership then encourages attacks in Europe and elsewhere to illustrate the organization's resilience.

IS activities differ from the state-sponsored terrorism that was a purported reason for the US attack on Saddam Hussein's Iraq in 2003. The theory at the time was that Saddam would provide terrorists with some of the WMD he was preparing and then dispatch those terrorists to wreak havoc on the United States and other countries he considered enemies. The flaws in that assumption soon became obvious, but what is important today is a terrorist organization such as IS does not need a sponsor. It is a "state" – albeit self-proclaimed – and decides on its own what it wants to target. It has its own civil and military infrastructure, including mechanisms to generate the income needed to support its attacks near and far. Although there has been limited public mention of IS acquiring WMD, it may well have the desire and capability to do so.

So, we have IS, a complex and sophisticated quasinational entity (more details about its operations in Chapter 3) that tightly controls those who work and live within it. We also have individuals directed and, perhaps more dangerous, inspired by IS and its brethren. These solo operators can do much damage on their own.

THE "LONE WOLVES"

First, some more definitions. The US Department of Homeland Security (DHS) distinguishes between "domestic terrorists" and "homegrown violent extremists." The former, states DHS, are those who commit a terrorist act and are "based and operating entirely within the United States or its territories without direction or inspiration from a foreign terrorist group." The National Counterterrorism

Center adds to this definition the proviso that the act is an attempt "to influence domestic policy." The 1995 bombing of the Oklahoma City federal building in which 168 people were killed and nearly 700 injured was domestic terrorism, as was the 2015 attack on a Colorado Springs Planned Parenthood Clinic. (By contrast, the assailant in the 2015 Charleston, South Carolina church shootings was charged not with domestic terrorism, but with murder and committing a federal hate crime. He was convicted and sentenced to death.) "Homegrown violent extremists," according to DHS, are those engaged in terrorist activities "in furtherance of political or social objectives promoted by a terrorist organization, but who [are] acting independently of direction by a terrorist organization."[24]

Thus, an attack such as the one in San Bernadino, California in 2015, in which the shooters were inspired by but not directed or trained by IS, would be homegrown violent extremism. Attacks such as those in Paris in 2015, in which the terrorists apparently received direction and training from IS, would fall outside these definitions.

The line between these two events, which is basically a question of when "inspired by" becomes "directed by," is fuzzy. Although the San Bernadino attackers, Tashfeen Malik and Syed Rizwan Farook, were not tied to IS in the way that the Paris killers were, they nevertheless had ingested much IS online content. Although the bloodshed was on a smaller scale, these were no less deadly than the Paris cohort.

As terrorism expert Peter Bergen has pointed out, "[E]very lethal jihadist terrorist attack in the U.S. since 9/11 has been carried out by individuals with no formal connection to foreign terrorist groups." These "lone wolves," wrote Bergen, "don't send emails or make calls that can be intercepted by the National Security

---

[24] Department of Homeland Security, "Countering Violent Extremism," October 14, 2015, www.dhs.gov/topic/countering-violent-extremism [accessed Februry 1, 2016]; National Counterterrorism Center, "Radicalization Dynamics: A Primer," June 2012, www.gangenforcement.com/uploads/2/9/4/1/29411337/radicalization_process.pdf [accessed January 30, 2015].

Agency or attend meetings with co-conspirators that can be detected by the FBI."[25]

Rather than being trained in Syria, Iraq, or other IS outposts, the homegrown terrorists are "self-radicalized." That term, however, may be misleading. Presumably rare is the homegrown terrorist who has thought through the justification and technique for committing a terrorist act solely on his or her own. These terrorists might have started along the path after reading a newspaper story about persecution of Muslims or other injustice somewhere in the world, but there are many steps between that initial stimulus and taking violent action. Taking those steps is enabled by the malignant media content that IS and other terrorist groups dispense in great quantity through the Internet.

The FBI reported that in 2015 it had conducted 900 investigations of militants in the United States.[26] Those were mostly people who turned out to have done nothing wrong, but those who deserved suspicion had made a tactical mistake, such as talking about plans for an attack to someone who proved to be an informant, or buying bomb components in a way that was reported. The smarter lone wolves are the most worrisome. The husband and wife killers in San Bernadino had been discreet. They practiced their marksmanship at a firing range, they amassed supplies of ammunition and explosives in their home, and they had a friend purchase a weapon for them, but all this stayed off the counterterrorism radar screens until after the fact. Their online communications were through personal e-mail, not public social media venues. Other than Malik's pledge on Facebook of her allegiance to IS, which she posted at the time of the shooting, there were no signals that the intelligence or law enforcement communities might have spotted.

That the San Bernadino couple could have truly been self-radicalized, using online material that they could discuss between

[25] Peter Bergen, "Can We Stop Homegrown Terrorists?," *Wall Street Journal*, January 23, 2016.
[26] Ibid.

themselves at the dinner table, underscores the menacing reality of lone-wolf terrorism. It also strengthens the case for more assertive CVE measures. In the San Bernadino case, perhaps local imams stressing that IS betrays, rather than strengthens, the values of Islam might have caused the attackers to rethink their plans. More generally, community leaders must be alert to incipient violence and be prepared to intervene. Especially among young people, extremist messaging must not be allowed to fester unchallenged.

But the simple fact is that terrorists produce so much online content that it can override even the most conscientious messaging by those who oppose extremism. This content includes skillful exhortations to commit violent acts as a religious obligation, such as the sermons (in Arabic and English) of the American-born Yemeni Anwar al-Awlaki, whose rhetoric has been found to have helped motivate numerous terrorists. Awlaki was killed by an American drone in 2011, but his online presence still looms.

Other sources of information and inspiration include the e-book, *How to Survive in the West: A Mujahid Guide.* Published in 2015, this book was disseminated through Twitter and other online venues by IS. It urged its readers to mount their own attacks and stated that with "an increasing amount of lone-wolf attacks, it will be more difficult for intelligence agencies to stop an increasing amount of violence and chaos from spreading in the West."[27]

For this kind of an attack, the goal of IS and others is to create maximum damage with minimum effort. The terrorist organizations spread the seeds of violence widely – Twitter is a good tool for this – and when one sprouts as an attack somewhere, the terrorist communicators claim responsibility and praise the attacker as their "soldier."

---

[27] Matthew Levitt, "The New York Bomber Was Not a Lone Wolf," September 21, 2016, http://foreignpolicy.com/2016/09/21/the-lone-wolf-era-is-over-new-york-islamic-state-ahmad-khan-rahani/ [accessed September 26, 2016].

When such attacks are publicized by mainstream media, they can give rise to "copycat" actions by those exposed to just the overall media environment in which stories about violence and political failures are pervasive. Knife attacks by Palestinians on Jewish Israelis have been carried out by lone wolves who don't need encouragement from Hamas or other terrorist groups. They are "terrorists" by most definitions, but they require little if any external stimulus beyond that provided by news reports, community conversation, and long-simmering personal frustration with their situation.

These individual acts are particularly frightening because they defy early detection. Beyond these instances of one-way communication designed to produce lone-wolf activity is the sophisticated recruitment process that relies heavily on social media conversation. As will be seen in Chapter 4, terrorist groups have proved highly skilled at enlisting long-distance adherents through online connections. If self-radicalization, as in the San Bernadino case, can produce such disastrous results, consider the effects of concerted radicalization efforts by terrorist trainers.

THE TERRORIST PROFILE

No uniform profile of "a terrorist" exists. During the early 1980s, West Germany conducted an exhaustive study attempting to determine why people become terrorists and to identify characteristics that could help counterterrorism agencies spot these people before an attack. The study failed to find definitive answers.[28] Similarly, the 9/11 Commission compiled detailed information about the airplane hijackers' backgrounds but found no common path toward radicalization.[29]

Terrorists' backgrounds vary, as do processes through which they are radicalized. Some, such as those who carried out the 9/11 attacks, have been parts of well-organized teams, trained and funded

---

[28] Crenshaw, Jenkins, and Hoffman, "How Much Really Changed?"
[29] The 9/11 Commission Report (New York: Norton, 2004), 160–65, 231–3.

by Al Qaeda, IS, or other groups. Some are motivated solely by sermons they hear or material they read on the Internet.

According to a 2016 BBC report, those who were part of the 2015 Paris attacks and who could be identified had some things in common, but in other ways were quite different. They ranged in age from twenty to thirty-one. Several were Belgian nationals and lived in the Molenbeek district of Brussels. One had worked as a technician for the Brussels tram system; one was a baker. Two others, brothers, had owned a bar and were known by locals as "big smokers and big drinkers" who "liked football, going clubbing, coming back with girls." One of these brothers was credited by neighbors with saving five children from a burning building. Almost all had had run-ins with law enforcement, mostly for petty offenses, and a number had been jailed. Several had been to Syria, presumably for IS purposes, and others had tried to get to Syria but had been blocked by authorities. Intelligence services apparently were aware of the activities of most members of the team, but had lost track of them.[30]

What stands out in the descriptions is the allure of the Syria-based caliphate and the ease of crossing borders. These men moved back and forth, only occasionally finding obstacles in their paths. The failure of intelligence and law enforcement agencies to keep track of them – even those known to be likely extremists – is mostly attributable to the number of such people moving between Europe and the Syria–Iraq war zone. This is frightening; even if they are blocked from entering Syria and sent home by a country such as Turkey, security services – in this case French and Belgian – do not have adequate resources to watch them all indefinitely. Sometimes extremists have been turned away from a European country only to return under different names and successfully enter.

Two of the Paris attackers apparently transited through the Greek island of Leros, posing as Syrian refugees. With several million

---

[30] "Paris Attacks: Who Were the Attackers?," BBC, January 19, 2016, www.bbc.com/news/world-europe-34832512 [accessed January 23, 2016].

Arab refugees on the move, many of them heading west into Europe, the threat of terrorist infiltration is a nightmare for security services and fodder for politicians who transform legitimate concerns about terrorism into sweeping anti-Arab sentiment and Islamophobia.

This influx of refugees is much more than a short-term crisis. The numbers are so large and the likelihood of most of the refugees ever returning home is so low that the economic and cultural characteristics of the places where they end up may be permanently changed. As this sinks in with the native populations in countries such as Germany and France, and in economically challenged Arab countries such as Jordan, political volatility will increase. When that happens, the risk of radicalization among the refugees may grow along with the cross-cultural tensions.

A 2015 RAND study found this risk to be shaped by a number of factors: "[T]he geographic placement and legal status of the refugees, the level of social and economic support for local populations in those locations, the preexistence of militant groups in refugee areas, and – perhaps more critical – the policies and actions of the receiving country, including its acceptance of militant organizations and its ability to provide security."[31] The study's authors wrote that they were "cautiously optimistic" because the international community had displayed foresight in its response to the recent refugees' needs for housing, schooling, and other essentials. This meant that the prospects for radicalization were somewhat reduced in comparison with, for example, the situation in refugee camps in the Democratic Republic of Congo after the 1994 Rwandan genocide or the camps in Lebanon during the 1970s and 1980s. In those instances, camps were controlled by radical groups and became bases for cross-border attacks.

Despite the relative calm today in camps and other areas with large concentrations of refugees, what will be the situation five or

---

[31] Barbara Sude, David Stebbins, and Sarah Weilant, "Lessening the Risk of Refugee Radicalization," *RAND Perspective*, 2015, 2, www.rand.org/pubs/perspectives/PE166.html [accessed February 3, 2016].

ten years from now? For many reasons, assimilation into non-Arab, non-Muslim societies may be difficult, and when the economic pressures related to the refugees' presence grow, local resentments may also increase. Such hostility, which may at least to some degree be religion based, will contribute to an atmosphere among the refugees that would be well suited for radicalization and recruitment. In this context, preventing the growth of violent extremism will be more difficult because advocates of radicalization will be appealing to a vulnerable constituency, its roots severed and prospects dismal.

As discouraging as the situation may seem to proponents of preventive counterterrorism, it is a time of boundless opportunity for IS and other extremist groups. As the disorientation that accompanied refugees' flight from the war zone dissipates, their frustration and anger will grow. Those in camps near the fighting are particularly tempting targets for extremist recruiters: "Cross the border and join the fight." Those farther away – in Western Europe and elsewhere – may be enlisted in terrorist plots where they are: "Get revenge against those who oppress our people and our religion."

Political leaders face the challenge of balancing a compassionate response to the refugee population with the dual responsibilities of keeping their own constituencies satisfied and safe, and ensuring that radicalization fails. These tasks, along with military and intelligence operations, are at the heart of counterterrorism.

Writing about radicalization, Shiraz Maher noted that when Mohammed Sidique Khan orchestrated the 2005 London bombings, he said he was doing so to retaliate for "the bombing, gassing, imprisonment, and torture of my people." But who were "my people"? Khan was born and educated in the United Kingdom, but, as Maher states, "he identified with the citizens of Iraq – a country he had not even traveled to and whose language he could not speak." This is a matter of identity, which has "long been recognized as being central to radicalization and not unique to Muslims ... The underlying ingredients are always the same: righteous indignation, defiance, a sense of persecution, and a refusal to conform," and they may lead to "violent – or at least confrontational – extremism."[32]

What might be called "identity drift" is partly a function of communication technologies that allow virtual connection to whatever "homeland" one considers to be his or her own. Everything from accessing that homeland's news media to joining online political communities can be accomplished easily through the Internet, contributing to a sense of belonging despite physical distance. But distance does matter, because knowledge of events and ideologies acquired in this way is, at best, second-hand. When someone like Mohammed Sidique Khan proclaims, "I am a soldier," his militancy has been nurtured not by on-the-ground training (which was the case with several of the 2015 Paris attackers), but rather through the radicalizing tools crafted by those who know that enlisting recruits and inspiring violent acts depend on the alluring arguments they can set forth in cyberspace. Those who want to prevent such recruitment will need to become far more adept at working within this same environment.

When considering the nature of the terrorist state and its "citizens," it is important to recognize that the definition of *state* is not carved in stone. Like much else in modern life, it is affected by new technologies, in this case primarily by communication tools that make physical contiguity less relevant to cohesion. These tools allow the virtual to transcend the physical, and IS, Al Qaeda, and other terrorist organizations have demonstrated that they know how to exploit this.

This is an essential element in understanding modern terrorism as a still-evolving phenomenon. IS and Al Qaeda are frightening enough in themselves, but if terrorism continues along its current path toward ever-greater organizational sophistication, the horrors that we know today may pale by comparison. Perhaps we will learn more about this from the testimonies of civilian survivors of Mosul

---

[32] Shiraz Maher, "The Roots of Radicalization? It's Identity, Stupid," *Guardian*, June 17, 2015.

and elsewhere where the singular act of terror has given way to a true reign of terror. This is why the terrorist state must be confronted.

Beyond the political roots of violent extremism is an even more powerful impetus for radical action: religion. The next chapter will show how some extremists depict themselves as agents of God. Some believe this, while others use professed religious commitment as a smokescreen to disguise mere thuggery. Whichever is the case, the result reflects the volatility of mixing politics and religion.

2   In God's Name

In the midst of bustling central London, there is a quiet spot between Fleet Street and the River Thames that is the Temple, home to Inns of Court and the Temple Church. The church was consecrated in 1185, and its design was based on that of the Church of the Holy Sepulcher in Jerusalem. This was the spiritual home of the Knights Templar, effigies of whom are to be found in the church. In the courtyard beside the church is a statue marking the departure point of English knights going to fight for Christian control of the Holy Land, keeping it out of the hands of the Saracens. "Saracen" was synonymous with "Muslim," and Knights Templar were also known as Crusaders.

The Crusades comprised successive military campaigns that lasted almost 400 years. This was promoted as "holy war," Christianity versus Islam. The ferocity of the Crusades still resonates, particularly in the Muslim world, where the word *crusade*, regardless of context, raises hackles.

The First Crusade was launched in 1095, and the Christian army moved into today's Middle East, slaughtering those who stood in its way. In 1099 the Crusaders captured Jerusalem and massacred the city's Muslim and Jewish inhabitants. Islamic forces slowly rebuilt their strength, and their leader Nur al Din, who wrote Amin Maalouf, had "a single objective, *jihad*, to reconquer the occupied territories and above all to liberate Jerusalem."[1] This goal was reached after Nur al-Din's death by his successor, the Kurdish warrior Saladin, who retook Jerusalem in 1187.

---

[1] Amin Maalouf, *The Crusades through Arab Eyes* (New York: Schocken, 1989), 144.

Control of the region's principal cities went back and forth between Western and Muslim armies for another century. All parties to the continuing conflict were intent on outdoing each other in the savagery directed at combatants and civilians alike. These horrific acts were justified by their perpetrators as being committed in the service of the Lord, even though the struggle for control of the region was also rooted in less-than-holy economic rivalries within and beyond Europe.

RELIGIOUS SEMANTICS AND PRINCIPLES

This history underscores the importance of understanding religion as part of the foundation of some forms of violent extremism, and of recognizing the role of religion in countering that extremism.

From the time of the Crusades, jump forward nearly a millennium; the warfare continues. Al Qaeda struck at America, considered to be the modern Crusader heartland, which had sent troops into Muslim countries during the 1991 Gulf War. When President George W. Bush used the word *crusade* in referring to his declaration of a "war on terror," Osama bin Laden quickly responded: "Our goal is for our [Muslim] nation to unite in the face of the Christian Crusade."[2]

Bin Laden and his colleagues recognized that they could expand their base of support by lifting their agenda above the politics of conflict and stressing the religious and cultural aspects of their efforts. French Foreign Minister Hubert Vedrine noted Bush's comment with alarm, seeing it as playing into bin Laden's hands. Vedrine said: "We have to avoid a clash of civilizations at all costs. One has to avoid falling into this huge trap, this monstrous trap ... conceived by the instigators of the assault."[3]

The trap Vedrine warned about is constructed through manipulation of Islam. Al Qaeda and other extremist Islamist groups have proved themselves adept at defining Islam and the content of

[2] Ibrahim, *The Al Qaeda Reader*, 272.
[3] Peter Ford, "Europe Cringes at Bush 'Crusade' Against Terrorists," *Christian Science Monitor*, September 19, 2001.

the Qur'an in ways that suit their purposes, and they have done so skillfully enough to overwhelm many opponents who endorse a more moderate Islam. The Qur'an, unlike the Bible, is not a collection of stories about God's works, but rather it is the direct word of God, as recited by God's messenger, the Prophet Mohammed. The Qur'an is therefore treated as not lending itself to diverse interpretation, and when there are disagreements about meaning, charges of apostasy quickly begin to fly. If an extremist course of action can be convincingly justified as fulfilling mandates found in the Qur'an, Muslim opposition to such action may wither.

But in practice, even the word of God means different things to different people, as do to particular terms. Consider *jihad*, which can be translated as "sustained struggle." According to some, this means a struggle within oneself to live according to the precepts of Islam, but others would say that it refers to an aggressive struggle against the enemies of Islam, a "holy war." Particularly in the West, the latter has been widely accepted as *jihad's* meaning, and *jihadist* is often used loosely as a synonym for "terrorist." Further, *jihad* can be viewed as both an individual and a collective duty, and so, if the community of Islam is attacked, all Muslims are required to join in *jihad* in response. But what is an "attack": combat such as that occurred during the Iraq War, or nonmilitary cultural encroachment by the West?[4]

The Qur'an can foster controversy. Consider this passage: "Fight in the cause of God those who fight you, but do not commit aggression: God loves not the aggressors ... Whoever commits aggression against you, retaliate against him in the same measure as he committed against you."[5] Muslim cultural critic Ziauddin Sardar observed that this is among the Qur'anic verses "bandied around by some Muslims to justify indiscriminate violence and by some non-Muslims to argue that Islam is inherently violent." Sardar added that the passage becomes a justification for violence only by "ignoring

---

[4] Youssef H. Aboul-Enein and Sherifa Zuhur, *Islamic Rulings on Warfare* (Carlisle, PA: Strategic Studies Institute, US Army War College, 2004), 4.

[5] Tarif Khalidi (trans.), *The Qur'an 2:190, 193* (New York: Viking, 2008), 26.

how this passage fits within the whole of the Qur'an's moral and ethical framework."[6] Taking a contrasting position, Al Qaeda leader Ayman al-Zawahiri cited that passage as part of the introduction to his treatise, "*Jihad*, Martyrdom, and the Killing of Innocents."[7]

In her study of IS's use of religion in its pronouncements, Theresa Ford noted that "87 percent of jihadist propaganda included justifications from the Qur'an, Hadith [words and actions of the Prophet Mohammed], or scholarship," and some of the group's statements cite the Qur'an dozens of times.[8]

Analyzing the Qur'an can be a life's work, and embarking on even part of that task would take us beyond the boundaries of this book. This brief discussion is only to illustrate the contrasting mores that shape the debate, and to point out how one can use one's own reading of the word of God to justify a vast range of actions.

Islam is certainly not the only religion relied upon by extremists. The gunman accused of killing three and wounding nine others at a Colorado Springs Planned Parenthood Clinic in 2015 had claimed to be a good Christian and had spoken of such attacks as being "God's work."[9]

His embrace of religion and violence was little different from that of the Muslim extremists who subscribed to the precepts of the IS and, just a few days after the Colorado killings, murdered fourteen and wounded twenty-one in San Bernardino, California. Jewish Israeli extremists have mounted terroristic attacks on Palestinians. Extremism in India has targeted Christians and Muslims. Violence between Buddhists and Muslims in Myanmar has killed hundreds. Catholic and Protestant extremists terrorized Northern Ireland for years. Anders Breivik, whose bomb and bullets killed seventy-seven people in Norway in 2011, was a Christian terrorist intent on

---

[6] Ziauddin Sardar, *Reading the Qur'an* (London: Hurst, 2015), 135–6.

[7] Ibrahim, *The Al Qaeda Reader*, 141.

[8] Theresa Ford, "How Daesh Uses Language in the Domain of Religion," *Military Review*, March/April 2016, 21.

[9] Richard Fausset, "For Robert Dear, Religion and Rage before Planned Parenthood Attack," *New York Times*, December 1, 2015.

galvanizing armed resistance against what he considered to be an insidious spreading of Islam in Europe. The list of incidents is depressingly lengthy and ecumenical, but today, because of the prominence and persistence of the IS, Al Qaeda, and their kin, counterterrorism efforts are primarily oriented to dealing with Muslim extremism.

Whatever their beliefs, and whether driven by reasoned malice or unreasoning insanity, many violent extremists wrap themselves in religion to disguise their destructiveness as something noble. Religion can never justify criminal irresponsibility on the part of individuals, organizations, or even nations. Nevertheless, religion and other aspects of culture cast broad shadows. Beyond individual acts are ramifications related to broad culture-based conflict, a "clash of civilizations."

THE CLASH

Harvard professor Samuel P. Huntington wrote an article for *Foreign Affairs* in 1993 titled "The Clash of Civilizations?" (Note the question mark.) In 1996, Huntington expanded this into a book, *The Clash of Civilizations and the Remaking of World Order* (without a question mark). At the heart of Huntington's argument, as stated in the book, is this: "In the post-Cold War world, the most important distinctions among peoples are not ideological, political, or economic. They are cultural." He added, "The rivalry of the superpowers is replaced by a clash of civilizations," and within the civilizations, "religion is a central defining characteristic."[10]

Although Huntington defined numerous cultures and situated them in a global context, much attention was given to Islam. The concept was not new. Middle East historian Bernard Lewis, in a 1990 lecture and magazine article, had discussed "a clash of civilizations" that was characterized in part by Muslim fundamentalists' "war against secularism" and "war against modernity."[11]

---

[10] Samuel L. Huntington, *The Clash of Civilizations and the Remaking of World Order* (New York: Simon and Schuster, 1996), 21, 28, 47.

[11] Bernard Lewis, *From Babel to Dragomans: Interpreting the Middle East* (New York: Oxford University Press, 2004), 329–30.

Debate about the concept attracted many, both supporters and critics. The criticism that resonated most was based on the idea that the true clash is not the Muslim versus non-Muslim world, but rather is occurring *within* Islam. Charles Kupchan observed that this struggle is the result of Muslim extremists manipulating the discontent that is prevalent in many Islamic countries. "The underlying source of alienation," he wrote, "is homegrown – political and economic stagnation and the social cleavages it produces."[12] Edward Said was sharply critical, calling Huntington's theory "preposterous." He argued that "cultures are hybrid and heterogeneous" and "so interrelated and interdependent" that they cannot be neatly matched up in a conflict scenario, one against another.[13]

The case for the existence of the clash resonates particularly among those who want to see battle lines drawn between Muslim and non-Muslim cultures. Although Huntington presumably did not envision his work being used this way, its argument has become a convenient tool for those who seek intellectual justification for cross-cultural violence. Once the idea of an inevitable clash is accepted, it becomes far easier politically to win approval for military or terroristic adventurism, whether it be a Western invasion of a Muslim country to preempt extremists or a jihadist attack to protect Islam.

Those who do not endorse violence may find the clash concept convenient politically. In France, the National Front (FN), led by Marine Le Pen, owes much of its support to its opposition to immigration and to Islam. Although some attribute FN's strength to economic nationalism, such as that behind the United Kingdom's "Brexit" movement, FN's Marion Marechal-Le Pen, an elected official and Marine Le Pen's niece, has said: "A father is afraid of his daughter wearing a burqa. It doesn't matter whether she will buy it with francs or euros." After the July 2016 terrorist attack in Nice that

---

[12] Charles A. Kupchan, *The End of the American Era* (New York, Knopf, 2002), 70.
[13] Edward W. Said, *Orientalism* (New York: Vintage, 2003), 347.

killed 86 and injured 434, Marechal-Le Pen said, "Christians must stand up to resist Islam."[14]

While the debate about Huntington's work has continued, his *Clash* has a far more violent counterpart: *The Management of Savagery*, written in 2004 by an Al Qaeda "theoretician" who called himself Abu Bakr Naji. (Naji was killed by a US drone strike in Pakistan in 2008.) It includes passages such as this: "Force America to abandon its war against Islam by proxy and force it to attack directly so that the noble ones among the masses and a few of the noble ones among the armies of apostasy will see that their fear of deposing the regimes because America is their protector is misplaced and that when they depose the regimes, they are capable of opposing America if it interferes."[15]

The common ground for the *Clash* and *Savagery* theories is just a narrow slice of terrain: that there is/will be a violent confrontation of some sort that transcends the current alignments of nation-states and ideologies. The conflict is instead grounded in religious-cultural competition. An element of this, noted Abdel Bari Atwan, is "the gruesome public exhibition of extreme violence [that] is part of a plan to instill fear and trepidation in the heart of the enemy."[16] IS-style executions by burning alive and beheading captives are examples of this.

The debate about Islam's future path in the world shows no signs of ending. It proceeds against a backdrop of demographic changes. A 2015 Pew Research Center survey found that between 2010 and 2050 the world's total population is expected to rise to 9.3 billion, a 35 percent increase. Over that same period, Muslims – a

---

[14] John Judis, *The Populist Explosion* (New York: Columbia Global Reports, 2016), 152.

[15] Abu Bakr Naji, *The Management of Savagery* (William McCants, trans.), https://thejihadproject.files.wordpress.com/2015/11/management_of_savagery.pdf, 24 [accessed January 23, 2016].

[16] Abdel Bari Atwan, *Islamic State: The Digital Caliphate* (Oakland: University of California Press, 2015), 164.

comparatively youthful population with high birth rates – are projected to increase by 73 percent. The number of Christians is also projected to rise, but more slowly – at about the same rate, 35 percent, as the global population overall. As a result, according to the Pew projections, by 2050 there will be near parity between Muslims (2.8 billion, or 30 percent of the population) and Christians (2.9 billion, or 31 percent). Further, Europe will be about 10 percent Muslim, up from just under 6 percent in 2010.[17] It should be noted that this latter figure does not reflect the effects of the large, present-day refugee flows from the Middle East into Europe. If not reversed at some point, these will further enlarge Europe's Muslim population.

But so what? Some assume that Europe will become an Islamized "Eurabia," with mosques appearing everywhere and an irresistible Muslim tide sweeping aside Christianity, Judaism, and other religions. But it may be, at least as likely, that many of the Muslims living in Europe will become Europeanized, with their religious practices shifting to conform to this new environment. No one really knows how the West's religious future will take shape. Furthermore, most clash-related discussions today are Europe- and Arab-centric, ignoring the more interesting – and perhaps more volatile – situation in sub-Saharan Africa, where the growth of both Islam and Christianity is strong and religious violence is growing. Also, Hindu–Muslim tensions in South Asia are always close to boiling and are particularly dangerous because the two dominant nations in the region, India and Pakistan, possess nuclear arsenals.

The significance of these trends will also depend on the evolution of political and economic environments in majority Muslim countries, especially those in the Middle East and South Asia. If rates of unemployment in much of the Arab world and the Indian subcontinent do not significantly improve, politics in those regions

[17] Pew Research Center, "The Future of World Religions: Population Growth Projections, 2010–2050," April 2, 2015, www.pewforum.org/2015/04/02/religious-projections-2010–2050/ [accessed March 1, 2016].

will become even more volatile and the generation that comes of age around 2050 will be unhappy and an attractive recruitment target for extremists. Further, as international mobility becomes easier, migration patterns may change and the population growth predicted in the Pew Research study may become more geographically dispersed.

The challenge, which must be addressed sooner rather than later, is to recognize these forthcoming changes in global religious balance and deal with the factors that could contribute to a clash that involves weapons rather than theories. Dealing with this must be done while being mindful that many extremists would like nothing better than to see a clash of civilizations become apocalyptic reality.

Further, the term *Muslim world*, while convenient, is something of a misnomer. It should not be taken as signifying uniformity. For one thing, Islam is divided: Sunni, Shia, Sufi, and numerous small sects, all perceiving their religion somewhat differently. Also, geography and culture make Islam heterogeneous. How much do the Muslim in Cairo, the Muslim in Lagos, the Muslim in Karachi, and the Muslim in Jakarta have in common? They may share the fundamentals of Islam, but even these are viewed through the lenses of their own very different lives. Islam is not a monolith, and this should be considered when contemplating any "clash" theory.

There are additional issues related to geography. Many national borders were created by conquerors who paid little heed to the realities of life on the ground. This is especially evident in the Arab world, beginning with the label "Middle East" – middle of what? – which was created, apparently, by British businessmen and an American naval strategist. More damaging were decisions by victorious powers after World War I that sliced up much of the Arab world in ways that left a legacy of dangerous incompatibility within the region.

Huntington died in 2008, but his work remains both provocative and valuable, regardless of whether one agrees with him. Relations among different cultures always feature a level of discomfort, but less certain is whether that necessarily leads to the kind of violent divisiveness that fosters terrorism.

ATTITUDES TOWARD RELIGION; ATTITUDES TOWARD VIOLENCE

Religion does not require fanaticism. That simple truth sometimes becomes lost when groups such as Al Qaeda and IS loudly proclaim ownership of a particular faith. The ferocity they bring to such a claim may make it believable, particularly by those who are intellectually distant from that particular religion.

It requires concerted effort to set aside stereotypes, particularly those rooted in fear. Speaking at Washington, D.C.'s Islamic Center a few days after the 9/11 attacks, President George W. Bush said: "These acts of violence against innocents violate the fundamental tenets of the Islamic faith ... The face of terror is not the true faith of Islam. That's not what Islam is all about. Islam is peace."[18]

Bush's visit to a mosque was important at a time when many in the United States felt comfortable demonizing all Muslims because of the actions of a handful of murderers. A predisposition against Islam existed, born largely of fear and ignorance. If the 9/11 terrorists had been of any other religion, would the president of the United States have felt it necessary to go to a church, temple, synagogue, or other place of worship to quell anger and fear? Almost certainly not.

Islamophobia remains dangerously close to the surface of life in the United States and numerous other countries, and it would probably not take much for it to burst forth, particularly because it is a convenient fuel for demagoguery, as could be seen during the 2016 US presidential campaign. This negative perception of Islam, however wrongheaded, works to the advantage of Islamic extremists. They try to provoke backlash against Muslims living in Europe, the United States, and elsewhere so they can point to such animosity as proof that Muslims need to come together and fight preemptively to ensure their survival. Only within a strong caliphate can Muslims,

---

[18] "'Islam Is Peace' Says President," Remarks at the Islamic Center of Washington, DC, September 17, 2001, http://georgewbush-whitehouse.archives.gov/news/releases/2001/09/20010917-11.html [accessed May 1, 2016].

according to the IS magazine *Dabiq*, "escape persecution from crusader governments and citizens."[19]

IS has proved skillful at nurturing antagonisms that serve its purposes and dominating elements of public discourse. Releasing videos that show children embarking on suicide bombing missions and other inflammatory content stokes the Islamophobia that extremist groups can turn to their advantage. With each news report about such violence, the backlash against Islam grows stronger.

Meanwhile, the countermessaging designed to undercut IS and other extremists struggles for credibility among Muslims who believe they must remain defensive against persecution. The most attention-getting measures are often ridiculous, such as the short-lived French ban on "burkini" swimsuits, but they reinforce Muslims' fears of discrimination and open the door to the "circle the wagons" exhortations from extremist groups.

MEASURING GLOBAL ATTITUDES

For non-Muslims to better understand Muslims, appreciating identity issues is important. At least in terms of the Arab world – which, remember, constitutes just 20 percent of the global Muslim population – how people see themselves is instructive in understanding the strength of religion in their lives. Surveys directed between 2004 and 2011 by Shibley Telhami explored whether people in the Arab Middle East identified themselves primarily by religion, nation, being Arab, or being a "citizen of the world." At the beginning of that period, the top three, in order, were "nation," "Muslim," and "Arab." By 2011, "Muslim" ranked first, "Arab" second, and nationality third. ("Christian," except in Lebanon, and "citizen of the world" remained far beneath the other three.) More striking is the change in responses to the question, "When your government makes decisions, do you think it should base its decisions mostly on what is best for Muslims, your country, Arabs, or the world?" In 2009, the

---

[19] Yaroslav Trofimov, "Islamic State Aims to Provoke Backlash Against Muslims in West," *Wall Street Journal*, December 10, 2015.

answers were "Muslims," 14 percent; "your country," 50 percent; "Arabs," 22 percent; and "the world," 4 percent. Within the span of a year, a significant shift took place. The 2010 results were "Muslims," 39 percent; "your country," 31 percent; "Arabs," 23 percent; and "the world," 5 percent. The results varied by country in expected ways, with strongest identity with religion in Saudi Arabia, and strongest identity with nationality in Lebanon, where nationhood is knitted together with complex and fragile stitching.[20]

These results were, to an extent, a foreshadowing of events in 2011, when the Arab uprisings reflected angry dissatisfaction with the performance of numerous Arab governments. Results of the uprisings were fleeting in terms of substantive positive change, but the dissatisfaction continues to smolder. Especially for young people, religion, rather than nationality, seems a better place to pin one's hopes. Bessma Momani observed: "For many youth who have a strong sense of faith in Islam, it is an attraction to principles of social justice that strengthens their identity as Muslims. With so much corruption and inequity surrounding them, religion provides a useful moral compass to redirect their energies and faith in society."[21]

On way for religion to be more ingrained in national life is through a country's laws. A Pew survey in 2015 in ten countries with significant Muslim populations found divided opinion about the extent to which the Qur'an should influence law. Pew reported that "in Pakistan, the Palestinian territories, Jordan, Malaysia, and Senegal, roughly half or more of the full population says that laws in their country should strictly follow the teachings of the Qur'an. By contrast, in Burkina Faso, Turkey, Lebanon, and Indonesia, less than a quarter agree."[22]

[20] Shibley Telhami, *The World through Arab Eyes* (New York: Basic Books, 2013), 27–34.

[21] Bessma Momani, *Arab Dawn: Arab Youth and the Demographic Dividend They Will Bring* (Toronto: University of Toronto Press, 2015), 73.

[22] Jacob Poushter, "The Divide over Islam and National Laws in the Muslim World," Pew Research Center, April 27, 2016.

This indicates the struggle that lies ahead. Can IS, by emphasizing its support for its approach to shariah-based governance, hijack the religious commitment of young Muslims and lure them to the purported caliphate? As we will see in Chapter 4, much of the IS media messaging is designed to do just that.

Although much of the world is dismayed by IS being able to attract tens of thousands of adherents to its cause, most of these young men and women are from fringe constituencies. Despite all the attention it garners with its claims to being the champion and protector of Islam, IS is viewed with disdain by most Muslims. A 2015 Pew Research Center survey in eleven countries with large Muslim populations found overwhelmingly "unfavorable" attitudes toward IS in Lebanon, Jordan, Palestine, Indonesia, and others. The country where the highest "favorable" rating was found was Nigeria, 14 percent, followed by Malaysia and Senegal, each with 11 percent. The same survey revealed, however, that IS had largely achieved its goal of spreading fear. In France (before the November 2015 attacks), 71 percent said they were very concerned about the IS threat, as did 77 percent of respondents in Spain, 70 percent in Germany, and 69 percent in Italy.[23]

European views of Muslims, as of early 2015, ranged from 19 percent "unfavorable" in Britain to 61 percent unfavorable in Italy. France and Germany were both 24 percent unfavorable, while Spain was 42 percent and Poland 56 percent unfavorable.[24]

The takeaway from such survey results is twofold. First, the IS methods of building its caliphate have negligible support within most of the *ummah*, the global Muslim community. But second, if non-Muslims' attitudes toward Islam drift toward greater

[23] Jacob Poushter, "In Nations with Significant Muslim Populations, Much Disdain for ISIS," Pew Research Center, November 17, 2015, www.pewresearch.org/fact-tank/2015/11/17/in-nations-with-significant-muslim-populations-much-disdain-for-isis/ [accessed February 12, 2016].

[24] Michael Lipka, "Muslims and Islam: Key Findings in the U.S. and Around the World," Pew Research Center, December 7, 2015, www.pewresearch.org/fact-tank/2015/12/07/muslims-and-islam-key-findings-in-the-u-s-and-around-the-world/ [accessed February 15, 2016].

negativity – which is particularly likely given the anti-Muslim political rhetoric in the United States, France, and elsewhere (especially the nasty brews bubbling on the Internet[25]) – cultural estrangement, if not an actual "clash," may hamper efforts to enlist the moderate Muslim community in efforts to counter violent extremism.

Although the West's outreach to the Muslim world has concentrated on Arab nations, long-term strategy must not neglect the countries with the biggest Muslim populations: Indonesia, India, Pakistan, Bangladesh, and Nigeria. More than 765 million Muslims live in these countries; that is almost half the world's total Muslim population and more than double the number of Arab Muslims.[26] Several of these countries are anything but serene; they have their own significant problems with extremism. But an optimistic view of them is that further development of their institutions of civil society and economic vitality would dampen extremism's appeal there. As Amin Maalouf observed, "Dynamic societies have a dynamic Islam, one that is innovative and creative; sluggish societies have a sluggish Islam, one that resists all change."[27]

SHAPING PERCEPTIONS

Much of this talk about Islam perpetuates the notion that it is the sole source of violent extremism. It isn't, of course; but particularly with the formerly high profile of Al Qaeda and the more recent rise of IS, terrorism rooted in what purports to be Islam is what people worry about. Abdul Rahman al-Rashad, editor of *Asharq Al-Awsat* newspaper, wrote in 2004, "It is a certain fact that not all Muslims are terrorists, but it is equally certain, and exceptionally painful, that almost all terrorists are Muslim." Referring to suicide

[25] For example, "Bare Naked Islam," www.barenakedislam.com/about/ [accessed August 1, 2016].

[26] www.pewforum.org/2015/04/02/muslims/pf_15-04-02_projectionstables74/ [accessed February 18, 2016].

[27] Amin Maalouf, *In the Name of Identity: Violence and the Need to Belong* (New York: Arcade, 2012), 64.

bombings, he added, "What a pathetic record. What an abominable achievement. Does this tell us anything about ourselves, our societies, our culture?"[28]

Al-Rashad's concern is understandable, but, as noted in the preceding chapter, terrorism is far from being a Muslim monopoly. Extremist attacks are not confined to any particular place, nor are they committed just by members of any particular religion. Ireland's IRA, Italy's Red Brigade, and Mexico's drug cartels are among the examples of non-Muslim extremist groups that in the not-too-distant past have embarked on terror campaigns.

That said, how many people outside the geographical base of such localized extremist organizations worry about being attacked by such groups? Part of the mission of Al Qaeda and IS is to spread fear – to terrorize – globally, and at this they have been exceptionally successful, even though their attacks have occurred in a limited number of locales. In 2014, the countries most affected by terrorism were Iraq, Afghanistan, Nigeria, Pakistan, and Syria, all of which are predominantly Muslim.[29] In addition to the perpetrators of most terrorist attacks being Muslim, so are most of their victims.

News coverage of this violence makes the distant seem proximate, and it infuses public discourse with not merely dismay but also worry that danger is not so far away. If it can happen in Kabul, why not here as well?

The Media Tenor news analysis firm found that in more than two-thirds of all news reports in 2015 about Muslim individuals and organizations, terrorism and violence were the main topics. This framing contrasted with that of Catholicism, which was largely positive because of the emphasis on Pope Francis. Coverage of Protestantism was more amorphous, which was due in part to the absence of a single figurehead and the sometimes complex relationships among

---

[28] John Kifner, "Massacre Draws Self-Criticism in Muslim Press," *New York Times*, September 9, 2004.
[29] www.start.umd.edu/pubs/START_GTD_OverviewofTerrorism2014_Aug2015.pdf [accessed March 2, 2016].

various denominations.[30] Islam has become a singular case, with the heart of its belief system, the work done by Islamic charities, and other positive attributes overshadowed by violence.

Stephen Pritchard, readers' editor of *The Guardian*, reported that "Islam is often wrongly portrayed as a single entity, and while broadsheets tend to feature reporting of Islam-related war and violence overseas, tabloids focus on fears about the 'Islamification' of the UK with particular focus on ... burkhas and immigration – the *Express*; violence – the *Mirror*; fanatics – the *Sun*; and halal meat and poppy-burning – the *Star*. Since 2010 there has been a small but significant increase in the positive portrayal of Muslim women, but the media continue to focus on them as victims. The main argument against the veil, for instance, has changed from one of the oppression of women to difficulties surrounding communication with the veil wearer," which included comparisons of veiled Muslim women to Darth Vader of *Star Wars*.[31]

News coverage – whether it is of religion, politics, or virtually any other topic – often sinks to the level of the lowest common intellectual denominator among its audience. Many people are fearful of and willing to dislike (or even hate) what they cannot understand. Some news organizations' penchant for sensationalism exacerbates this. Such is particularly the case when players such as IS know enough about how the news media work to be able to manipulate superficial public perceptions. In coverage of matters related to religion, violence trumps prayer.

A further matter to keep in mind about news coverage of extremism: not all terrorist attacks are reported in the same way; biases, often unintentional, may intrude. The November 13, 2015 attacks in Paris that left 130 persons dead received intensive, continuing coverage from the world's news media, with descriptions citing

[30] http://us.mediatenor.com/en/library/newsletters/798/terror-and-fear-shape-the-image-of-islam [accessed March 28, 2016].

[31] Stephen Pritchard, "The Readers' Editor on ... Islam and the Media," *Guardian*, September 27, 2015, www.theguardian.com/world/2015/sep/27/reader-editor-on-islam-media [accessed March 18, 2016].

"disbelief, panic" and a "massacre." Social media discourse featured outpourings of sympathy from the public, with many on Facebook using a superimposed French flag on their postings. The day before, in Beirut, an IS bombing killed 43 and wounded more than 200, and a typical Western headline was *Slate's* "Dozens Killed in Bombing Targeting Hezbollah Stronghold in Lebanon." Although civilians were victims in Lebanon as they were in France, much of the coverage highlighted the location's purported connection to Hezbollah. This framing implicitly categorized the attack as "just another example of Middle East violence," and as being particularly easy to dismiss because the victims were Arabs. Nadine Ajaka wrote that "it's difficult to make the argument that the media landscape we all stumble through is anything approaching equitable – or to avoid the impression that white victims are being humanized in a way Arab victims aren't. It is through language that the press shapes political discourse, and it is through language that our biases are made manifest."[32]

Political rhetoric tilted much the same way as the news reporting did. After the Paris attacks, US Senator Lindsey Graham said, "This is not just an attack on the French people, it is an attack on human decency and all we hold dear."[33] True enough. But, as David Graham observed, "American politicians issued few equivalent statements about Beirut. If no one points out that suicide bombings in Beirut are no less an attack on human decency than those in Paris, it is much easier to sort the world into a clash of civilizations – where innocent deaths on one side are more deserving of mourning than innocent deaths on the other."[34]

[32] Nadine Ajaka, "Paris, Beirut, and the Language Used to Describe Terrorism," *Atlantic*, November 17, 2015, www.theatlantic.com/international/archive/2015/11/paris-beirut-media-coverage/416457/ [accessed January 12, 2016].

[33] www.lindseygraham.com/2015/11/14/on-hugh-hewitt-and-nbcs-today-show-graham-responds-to-terror-attacks-in-paris-with-plan-to-defeat-isil/ [accessed January 10, 2016].

[34] David A. Graham, "The Empathy Gap between Paris and Beirut," *Atlantic*, November 16, 2015, www.theatlantic.com/international/archive/2015/11/paris-beirut-terrorism-empathy-gap/416121 [accessed January 23, 2016].

IN GOD'S NAME 63

For many people, perceptions of extremism and the best ways to respond to it are at least partially shaped by popular media, especially television and cinema. American movies in the "terrorism" genre include *The Siege* (1998), which features terrorist attacks in New York leading to martial law and prison camps for Muslims, and *Zero Dark Thirty* (2012), which seems to some viewers to endorse the use of torture, such as waterboarding, by US intelligence agencies. The list is long and the quality of the films as "entertainment" is varied.

One of the most controversial (and most popular) homes for counterterrorism exploits was the television program *24*, which aired between November 2001 and May 2010, pitting US government operative Jack Bauer against an array of terrorists. As Jane Mayer noted about the show, Bauer and his team frequently employed extreme coercion when confronting suspected evildoers: "With unnerving efficiency, suspects are beaten, suffocated, electrocuted, drugged, assaulted with knives, or more exotically abused; almost without fail, these suspects divulge critical secrets." Mayer cited the Parents' Television Council as having identified sixty-seven torture scenes during *24*'s first five seasons, and she wrote that in the show's plotlines: "Nobody argues that torture doesn't work, or that it undermines America's foreign-policy strategy. Instead, the doubters tend to be softhearted dupes." Eventually, the real world intruded. Senior US military officers told the show's producers that *24* was having a toxic effect – that it "promoted unethical and illegal behavior and had adversely affected the training and performance of real American soldiers" in places such as Iraq, where DVDs of the show were widely shared among US troops.[35]

When producers of *24* were urged to be more cautious in showing depictions of illegal tactics employed by the program's "heroes," their reaction was, "C'mon; it's only a television show." That was

---

[35] Jane Mayer, "Whatever It Takes," *New Yorker*, February 19, 2007, www.newyorker.com/magazine/2007/02/19/whatever-it-takes [accessed January 28, 2016].

disingenuous given the size of the audience (more than 13 million viewers per episode during several seasons) and the amount of extraneous attention *24* received. Popular culture can be a significant factor in shaping public perceptions about many topics, ranging from hair styles to sex to religion. Response to violent extremism is no exception. And when the storylines implicitly or explicitly portray Muslims as the worst villains, once again the "clash" concept gains traction.

Moral obtuseness in addressing torture does not strengthen efforts against terrorism. Beyond television programs, when the world hears American presidential candidates proclaim support for measures more violent than waterboarding, leaders of groups such as Al Qaeda and IS are certainly delighted. They don't need to make the case about Western hatred of Islam because it is being done for them.

RESPONDING THROUGH RELIGION

As logical as it might seem to address religious issues through policies articulated in a religious context, complications arise primarily because some governments are wary about entering this terrain. These same governments might not be gun-shy when putting armed force behind their policies, but they are what we might call "God-shy."

US Secretary of State Madeleine Albright is among those who have most directly addressed such matters, noting that foreign policy "requires a clear grasp of what matters most to those we are trying to influence." She cited Catholic theologian Bryan Hehir, who observed "There is an assumption that you do not have to understand religion to understand the world. You need to understand politics, strategy, economics, and law, but you do not need to understand religion. If you look at standard textbooks of international relations or the way we organize our foreign ministry, there's no place where a sophisticated understanding of religion as a public force in the world is dealt with."[36]

---

[36] Madeleine Albright, *The Mighty and the Almighty: Reflections on America, God, and World Affairs* (New York: Harper Perennial, 2007), 11, 66.

Albright added that many foreign policy practitioners "have sought to separate religion from world politics, to liberate logic from beliefs that transcend logic."[37] Especially in US policy-making circles, this intellectual premise is bolstered by the perception that the constitutional mandate for the separation of church and state extends into foreign policy. This is incorrect; the First Amendment provision – "Congress shall make no law respecting an establishment of religion, or prohibiting the free exercise thereof" – does not preclude relying on elements of religion in relations with the rest of the world. Nevertheless, hesitancy lingers, putting US policy toward many peoples at a disadvantage.

Jennifer Marshall and Thomas Farr wrote that "a lack of appreciation for how religion can buttress and expand ordered liberty leads to a lack of vocabulary, imagination, and remedies that draw on religious ideas, individuals, and institutions. When U.S. policy communicates an official position of awkwardness and reticence on these matters, and ambivalence about the significance of religion in people's lives, it hinders U.S. policymakers from reaching and winning hearts and minds abroad."[38] As a corrective measure, Albright urged that "the State Department should hire or train a core of specialists in religion to be deployed both in Washington and in key embassies overseas," and further suggested that each US embassy include a religion attaché on its staff.[39]

All these points underscore the necessity of systemic changes within the foreign policy establishments of the United States and, to varying degrees, in those of other Western nations. These may be difficult to accomplish, however, partly because of the politicization of religion as it relates to violent extremism. This cuts two ways.

[37] Ibid., 73.
[38] Jennifer A. Marshall and Thomas F. Farr, "Public Diplomacy in an Age of Faith," in Philip Seib (ed.), *Toward a New Public Diplomacy: Redirecting U.S. Foreign Policy* (New York: Palgrave Macmillan, 2009), 199.
[39] Albright, *The Mighty and the Almighty*, 76; www.pbs.org/wnet/religionandethics/episodes/may-19–2006/madeleine-albright/1845/ [accessed January 28, 2016].

Some politicians simplistically excoriate Islam, as if all the world's 1.6 billion Muslims were terrorists. Others handle the issue, and particularly its terminology, too gingerly. They refuse, for example, to use the term *radical Islam*, and instead substitute obfuscations such as "radical jihadist ideology." As Kim Ghattas observed, the debate fractures further, with some Muslims appreciating attempts to disconnect radical ideology from their religion, while others say that if the issue is seen as non-Islamic, then thoughtful consideration of the state of Islamic thought is less likely to take place.[40] These matters, particularly their ugliest features, were on full display during the 2016 US presidential campaign, with some candidates discussing the unfitness of Muslims to be president or even to enter the country. Similar statements have become increasingly common in some Western European political circles. During the presidency of Donald Trump, it is likely that the US government will attempt to enact anti-Muslim measures related to immigration and perhaps other matters.

Such rhetoric and actions put pressure on Muslims. The Morocco-born novelist Laila Lalami, who lives in the United States, wrote, "To be a Muslim in the West is to be constantly on trial." She added that those who espouse anti-Muslim sentiments are aiding the IS ideologues who want "to eliminate coexistence between religions and create a response from the West that will force Muslims to choose sides": Either adopt "the infidel religion" or remain Muslim and escape to the IS caliphate.[41]

Later in this book, we will examine Western programs for discouraging potential IS recruits, a process that must touch many aspects of these individuals' lives. But for now, it is safe to conclude that much of the explicit and implicit religion-related rhetoric emanating from the non-Muslim West – especially from the United States – is, at best, counterproductive. It fails to offset portrayals of

[40] Kim Ghattas, "The Democrats' Problem with 'Radical Islam,'" *Foreign Policy*, November 27, 2015, http://foreignpolicy.com/2015/11/27/the-democratic-problem-with-radical-islam [accessed November 28, 2015].
[41] Laila Lalami, "My Life as a Muslim in the West's 'Gray Zone,'" *New York Times Magazine*, November 20, 2015.

Muslims as victims needing a rescuer, however extreme. This bias, intentional or not, reinforces the IS argument that Western civilization is intrinsically hostile toward Islam and therefore only fierce militancy can provide hope and protection.

Counterextremism efforts are most likely to be successful when they involve Muslims speaking to Muslims. This is more difficult than it may at first seem because within Islam competing voices endorse different paths toward the future. Among those at the center of such discussions are the imams at individual mosques, but they are far from uniform in their views. Tunisia provides an example of the difficulties of advancing religious moderation.

The "Arab spring" began in Tunisia. In December 2010, Mohamed Bouazizi, a former university student who was trying to eke out a living by selling fruits and vegetables, was victimized by corrupt officials in his hometown, Sidi Bouzid, a city of about 40,000 in central Tunisia. Overwhelmed by despair about his future, Bouazizi went to the governor's office, shouted "How do you expect me to make a living?," poured paint thinner over himself, and lit a match.

While Bouazizi lay dying in a hospital, his family and friends organized an angry protest outside the governor's office. Bouazizi's cousin posted a video of the protest on YouTube, and it was picked up by Al Jazeera and other broadcasters.[42] As the video was played and replayed on channels outside the control of the Tunisian government, demonstrations around the country picked up steam. President Zine el-Abidine Ben Ali, who had ruled Tunisia since 1987, fled to Saudi Arabia. Broadcasts and social media delivered news of the events in Tunisia throughout the Arab world and the so-called Arab spring was underway.

Many radical, Salafist Tunisian clerics had been jailed during the Ben Ali years. Most were released through a postrevolution

[42] Robin Wright, *Rock the Casbah: Rage and Rebellion across the Islamic World* (New York: Simon and Schuster, 2011), 16. See also, Philip Seib, *Real-Time Diplomacy: Politics and Power in the Social Media Era* (New York: Palgrave Macmillan, 2012), 17–18.

amnesty, and they quickly reasserted themselves, taking control of several hundred mosques. In 2013, the new Tunisian government began monitoring the country's mosques and replacing violence-inciting clerics, but with approximately 5,400 mosques in the country, attempts at control were only partially successful. Further, the radicals pointed to the government's efforts as evidence of "true believers" being persecuted.

To strengthen the position of moderate imams, Tunisia looked to Morocco, where counterradicalization efforts had been spurred by a string of terrorist attacks. Reforms have included creation of television and radio channels that carry programs emphasizing religious tolerance. This message is also delivered in the country's mosques, with care to avoid relying too heavily on simplistic rhetoric, such as "Islam is a religion of peace." Without being supported by more sophisticated argumentation, that premise is susceptible to being undermined by the radicals. Generational issues also come into play, as the restive youth of Tunisia, Morocco, and other Arab countries are skeptical about their elders' pleas for patience during the political and economic reform process.[43]

A popular expression in the American political world is, "All politics is local." A similar statement can be made about religion: "All religion is local." In the Muslim world, whether in a tiny village or a big city, the mosque is at the center of the community and is influential in shaping religious thought among many members of the public. This influence is not uniform. As with other religions, many Muslims, especially among the young, have grown disenchanted with the religious establishment, even if they have not drifted away from Islam, and they look to sources other than the local imam for guidance on religious matters. (Some television and online Muslim "televangelists" have built huge followings.) By

[43] Christine Petre, "How Tunisia's Moderate Imams Are Seeking to Reclaim Islam from Extremists," *Al-Monitor*, December 8, 2015, www.al-monitor.com/pulse/originals/2015/12/tunisia-mosques-efforts-reclaim-islam-jihadis-radicalism.html# [accessed February 1, 2016].

contrast, some young people, dissatisfied with their lives, flock to mosques that deliver messages designed to radicalize. Regardless of the content of mosques' teachings, working at the grassroots level – in mosques and madrasas (religious schools) – must be integral to anti-extremist efforts.

Outside the Arab world, the dynamics of Islam are also changing. In Niger, Nigeria, Somalia, and other African countries, poverty and poor governance have led many to look beyond traditional religious practices, which for African Muslims had often centered on Sufi Islam. Now, proselytizing by Sunni charities funded by Saudi Arabia has contributed to a more radical religiosity. Africans are brought to Saudi institutions such as the Islamic University of Medina and then return as imams at Saudi-built mosques in their home countries. Their embrace of Wahhabi theology has contributed to the growth of groups such as Boko Haram in Nigeria, which has declared its home turf to be the "West Africa Province" of IS.[44]

Although the historic Muslim homeland is in the Arab world, the true Muslim heartland today is in South and East Asia, where the Muslim population dwarfs that of the Middle East. (This region has about a billion Muslims, 62 percent of the world's total, compared to approximately 340 million, 22 percent of the global Muslim population, in the Middle East.) This has not been lost on IS recruiters. They proselytize on social media and urge young East Asians to come join in building the caliphate. IS has created a brigade of its fighters for Indonesians and Malaysians. As with sub-Saharan Africa, Muslim-majority countries in East Asia have seen considerable growth in foreign-funded religious schools, and the region's poorly administered prison systems have also fostered radicalization. Add to this the Islamophobia that has led to violence in Muslim-minority countries such as Myanmar, providing still more incentive for Muslim radicalization.

[44] Yaroslav Trofimov, "Jihad Comes to Africa," *Wall Street Journal*, February 5, 2016.

A key factor in moving in the *other* direction – away from extremism – is responsive government. Indonesia is relatively democratic, allowing considerable free expression and vesting enough power in decentralized government to allow voters who are devoutly religious to achieve their political goals at the local level (including enforcement of shariah law in Aceh province). This reduces impetus for having a national extreme Islamist party, although the Prosperous Justice Party, which has won more than 8 million votes in legislative elections, has ties to the Arab world's Muslim Brotherhood.[45] Evidence of the reluctance to embrace extremist views can be seen in the Pew Research survey finding that 79 percent of Indonesian respondents had an unfavorable view of IS.[46]

Despite these indications of support for a relatively low-key approach to Islam, some warning signs have emerged from the Aceh experiment in containing the more radical outlook. As Jon Emont reported, "In Aceh, women are required to dress modestly, alcohol is prohibited, and numerous offenses – from adultery to homosexuality to selling alcohol – are punishable by public whipping." Even though Banda Aceh, the province's capital, has elected a woman mayor, she has proved, wrote Emont, "a zealous, hands-on enforcer of Aceh's conservative moral code, issuing a nighttime curfew for women and personally dispersing events deemed to contradict Shariah." Emont also cited a study that found that since 1999, when the Indonesian government gave provinces and districts greater authority to make their own laws, more than 442 shariah-based ordinances had been passed throughout the country.[47]

[45] Joshua Kurlantzick, "Democratic Regression and the Rise of Islamic State-Linked Militants in Southeast Asia," Council on Foreign Relations, February 4, 2016, http://blogs.cfr.org/asia/2016/02/04/democratic-regression-and-the-rise-of-islamic-state-linked-militants-in-southeast-asia/ [accessed February 7, 2016].

[46] Jacob Poushter, "In Nations with Significant Muslim Populations, Much Disdain for ISIS," Pew Research Center, November 17, 2015, www.pewresearch.org/fact-tank/2015/11/17/in-nations-with-significant-muslim-populations-much-disdain-for-isis/ [accessed February 9, 2016].

[47] Jon Emont, "As Shariah Experiment Becomes a Model, Indonesia's Secular Face Slips," *New York Times*, January 12, 2017.

Indonesia is also home to the world's largest independent Islamic organization, Nahdlatul Ulama (NU), translated as "revival of religious scholars," which has 50 million members and has pushed back hard against IS doctrine. An NU film shows IS soldiers executing prisoners and, instead of the usual triumphant IS voiceover, this version has commentary from former Indonesian president Abdurrahman Wahid, singing a Javanese poem: "Many who memorize the Qur'an and Hadith love to condemn others as infidels while ignoring their own infidelity to God, their hearts and minds still mired in filth."[48]

NU is building a "prevention center" in Indonesia to train Arabic-speaking students to counter rhetoric from Muslim extremists, local and distant. Working with Muslim clerics, NU is also helping to mobilize 50,000 imams to spread a moderate form of Islam within Indonesia.[49] With such efforts, plus the sheer size of NU and Indonesia's overall Muslim population of roughly 223 million, it may make sense to look to Indonesia as a model foil to IS global growth aspirations and to adapt the Indonesian message of moderation to appeal to the larger world of Islam.

Any long-term effort to undercut violent extremism must address reform of Islamic teaching. In many of the world's Islamic schools, the curriculum is narrow, embracing Salafist-like doctrine without nurturing critical thinking. Instruction in these schools goes no farther than rote memorization of the Qur'an.

The backwardness of this approach is not lost on some of those who have gone through this schooling. One former recruiter for the radical group Hizb ut-Tahrir said of his education: "What I understood to be the correct reading of Islam was in fact just one of many historical interpretations that existed out there. The theological pluralism

[48] Joe Cochrane, "From Indonesia, a Muslim Challenge to the Ideology of the Islamic State," *New York Times*, November 26, 2015.
[49] Krithika Varagur, "World's Largest Islamic Organization Tells ISIS to Get Lost," *Huffington Post*, December 3, 2015, www.huffingtonpost.com/entry/indonesian-muslims-counter-isis_us_565c737ae4b072e9d1c26bda [accessed February 20, 2016].

that used to exist has been lost among angry young Muslims."
A former member of the Taliban said about teaching the Qur'an: "Of
course I believe it is the word of God ... but my counterargument is
this: Do you think God is confined to the sociopolitical culture of the
700s? ... When the Qur'an says, 'Prepare your steeds for war,' this is
one of the exhortations to military readiness. How come you inter-
pret that to mean today it's tanks and machine guns? Why aren't you
using swords and spears and shields?"[50]

A leader in reforming Islamic schools – madrasas – has been
the Washington, D.C.-based International Center for Religion and
Diplomacy (ICRD), directed by former US Navy officer Douglas
Johnston. ICRD works on numerous issues related to religion and
peacemaking, and in education it has done much in Pakistan, which
is home to roughly 20,000 madrasas. The main goals of the ICRD
efforts have been to expand curricula to include physical and social
sciences (with particular emphasis in the latter on religious tolerance and women's rights), and to change pedagogy in ways that will
encourage students to ask questions and develop their own viewpoints about the schools' subject matter. ICRD has worked with
about 2,500 Pakistani madrasas and has been successful in encouraging some madrasa leaders to organize the reforms themselves and
incorporate Islamic principles in the process. As the project matured,
Pakistani universities were enlisted to play a larger role in teacher
training and curriculum reform.[51]

In Pakistan, the madrasas are not alone in being problematic
in terms of reducing extremist influence. Public education has long
been a low priority for the Pakistani government, with students being
expected to memorize the names of the country's military heroes
and sayings of the Prophet Mohammed, but not learning algebra or

---

[50] "How to Beat ISIS: Reform Islamic Teaching," *New York Times*, November 17,
2015.
[51] Douglas M. Johnston, "Madrasa Reform in Pakistan," speech at the Woodrow
Wilson International Center for Scholars, October 8, 2014, icrd.org/wp-content/
uploads/Madrasa-Reform-in-Pakistan-Final-Transcript.pdf [accessed Fe ruary 27,
2016].

biology. Some teachers are paid the equivalent of US$50 per month, and a 2006 study found that more than 50 percent of Pakistan's public schools did not have electricity. This situation may be part of an effort by the economically and politically dominant class to preserve the status quo by denying the lower classes the education they would need to rise. Meanwhile, children of the country's elite attend excellent private schools.[52]

Extremist groups, such as the Pakistani Taliban, have turned some schools into battlefields. In Peshawar in 2014, the Taliban assaulted a school and killed more than 130 children. Education for young women attracts particular attention from extremists, as was evidenced by the attempted murder in 2012 of Malala Yousafzai, a champion of girls' education who went on to win the Nobel Peace Prize. This issue is just one facet of gender issues that are carried to violent extremes by extremist groups, which are abetted by the religious establishment. Again in Pakistan, a law passed in Punjab in early 2016 that would protect women from violence was promptly declared "un-Islamic" by some mullahs.[53]

In East Asia, the number of religious schools has gradually grown smaller. In Indonesia, for example, religious schools – *pesantren* – date back to the sixteenth century and about 13,000 were operating as the twenty-first century began. But as public education has improved, many Muslim parents prefer those government-run schools, which offer curricula that they believe will best prepare their children for the job market.[54]

Addressing another facet of public schools' role, Rached Ghannouchi, leader of Tunisia's Ennhada movement, suggested to the French government that it set up its own Islamic schools that would instill secular as well as religious values. Such schools could

[52] Griff Witte, "Poor Schooling Slows Anti-Terrorism Effort in Pakistan," *Washington Post*, January 17, 2010.
[53] "A Game of Dare," *Economist*, March 5, 2016, 37.
[54] Howard M. Federspiel, "Pesantren," in *The Oxford Encyclopedia of the Islamic World, Oxford Islamic Studies Online*, www.oxfordislamicstudies.com/article/opr/t236/e0632 [accessed March 1, 2016].

also limit the number of young people exposed to the teaching of radical doctrine.[55]

Education issues might, at first glance, seem far removed from counterterrorism, but Islam pervades the lives of Muslims in so many ways that the only means of creating realistic measures to undermine extremism is to recognize that episodic efforts are far inferior to systemic reforms. The latter take time and money, and they do not provide the gratification (for some) of watching a cruise missile do its work. But extremism's pervasive effects will be diminished only if societal change occurs, with incremental progress in the Muslim world and concurrent shifts in attitudes elsewhere that reduce Islamophobia and other barriers to tolerance.

Those who devise and implement strategies for confronting terrorism must recognize that when religion becomes politicized – and even weaponized – to the extent that we see today, extremism will develop stronger roots. As those roots grow deeper, they nourish the evolution of terrorism.

---

[55] Robert F. Worth, *A Rage for Order* (New York: Farrar, Straus and Giroux, 2016), 219–20.

3 Organizing Terrorism

Terrorism's longevity is attributable in part to its ability to adjust to changing political and technological environments. A terrorist "organization" was once the semi autonomous cell of Joseph Conrad's *The Secret Agent*, a novel based on a nineteenth-century attempt to blow up London's Greenwich Observatory. As Conrad said, these terrorists received occasional instructions from the embassy of an unnamed country, and members of the cell communicated with each other only sporadically. As practitioners, they were disastrously inept.

Over the years, terrorists and their organizations became more sophisticated and their actions conformed to the societal milieu of the moment, especially as related to media. During the later decades of the twentieth century, the prospect of television coverage proved irresistibly alluring to terrorists. At the 1972 Munich Olympic Games, the Black September Palestinian terrorist group invaded the dormitory that housed Israeli athletes, killing several and taking others hostage while demanding the release of prisoners held by Israel and Germany. A rescue attempt failed, and the episode ended with seventeen dead: eleven Israeli athletes and coaches, a West German police officer, and five of the terrorists. Much of this transpired within view of the television cameras that were on site for the Olympics, and the world watched, transfixed, as events played out.

The three surviving terrorists were captured and imprisoned, only to be released the following month after Black September struck again, hijacking a Lufthansa passenger jet and demanding that their compatriots be set free. After this, Israeli Prime Minister Golda Meier authorized "Operation Wrath of God," which involved tracking down and killing Black September fighters. During the next few years, there were back-and-forth assassinations between the Israelis and the Palestinians. The cycle doesn't end; terrorism's violence breeds more violence.

During the 1980s, airplane hijackings were in vogue. They were not particularly difficult to accomplish and generated plenty of media exposure. Some were bloody, some were not. Some achieved the goals, such as the release of prisoners, and some accomplished nothing beyond a brief spurt of publicity. During these hijackings, most of the passengers and aircraft survived. At that time, using the aircraft for attacks, as happened on September 11, 2001, was beyond imagination.

Even the events attracting the most public attention produced merely small victories for their perpetrators. The media coverage often turned their efforts into circuslike distractions that had little lasting impact. In the aftermath of one hijacking, the terrorists decided to show off their hostages at a news conference, during which the journalists became so rowdy that the terrorists had to fire their weapons in the air to restore order. The hijackings, bombings, and assassinations rarely, if ever, created terror that spread to large portions of a population or significantly affected governments' policy makers.

During the past twenty years, terrorism has become very different. For one thing, the frequency and severity of terrorist acts has increased. Writing immediately after the March 2016 bombings in Brussels, Sohrab Ahmari observed that "Islamic terrorism is now a permanent and ubiquitous hazard to life in every city, on every continent ... Not a single day now goes by without an Islamist suicide bombing, rocket attack, shooting, spree, kidnapping or stabbing somewhere in the world." Ahmari presented a list of attacks that had occurred during the previous ten days and noted, "You could create a calendar like this one that stretches back for weeks and months, and the above doesn't even include the civil wars and humanitarian calamities in Iraq, Syria, Libya, and Afghanistan."[1] Add the terroristic acts committed by non-Muslims to the incidents of what Ahmari calls "Islamic terrorism" and his calendar would be even

---

[1] Sohrab Ahmari, "Global Jihad's Deadly Calendar," *Wall Street Journal*, March 23, 2016.

more crowded. With terror so commonplace, a bombing today that kills dozens but occurs far away does not even rate space on a newspaper's front page.

Another major change is that the terrorist community has become more densely populated. Terror operations are most often conducted by organizations with distinct identities that try to outdo one another in their quests for notoriety. The key word is *organizations*, which in many cases have become complex in structure and sophisticated in their activities. The leading "brands" in the world of terrorists compete for allegiance, money, and political support from those who find their efforts appealing.

Perhaps the most striking change emerging from terrorism's evolution is that some of the larger and more organizationally advanced terror groups are seizing territory and creating formalized mechanisms of governance. Terror remains at the heart of the political identity of these quasistates, and as will be seen later in this chapter, the lives of people inhabiting these realms are dominated by fear and coercion.

The evolving terrorist organization has institutionalized the worst aspects of society. It has reversed human progress.

THE MULTIPOLAR TERRORIST WORLD

As of early 2017, the world's dominant terrorist organization – in terms of damage inflicted and publicity received – is IS, which, according to the International Crisis Group, "has reshaped the jihadist landscape." A Crisis Group report stated that IS "has woven together sectarian, revolutionary, and anti-imperialist threads of jihadist thought. Its leadership is mostly Iraqi but the movement is protean: millenarian and local insurgent; to some a source of protection, to others of social mobility, and yet others of purpose; with strands aiming to consolidate the caliphate, take Baghdad or even Mecca, or lure the West into an apocalyptic battle."[2]

---

[2] International Crisis Group, "Exploiting Disorder: Al-Qaeda and the Islamic State," executive summary, March 14, 2016, www.crisisgroup.org/en/regions/global/exploiting-disorder-al-qaeda-and-the-islamic-state.aspx [accessed March 21, 2016].

As we will see, the *perception* of IS's dominance might be due, at least partly, to flash rather than substance. In terms of long-term adaptability and survivability, Al Qaeda should not be underestimated. And in terms of pure viciousness, IS is on occasion outdone by Boko Haram and others.

The terrorists who merit most attention from counterterrorism policy makers are not those in ragtag groups with little organizational infrastructure, although even they can sporadically wreak much havoc with simple weapons and explosives. Of greatest concern are the organizations that aspire to permanence through establishing a "states" – called a "caliphate," "emirate," or something else – real or virtual.

IS and other terrorist bodies have, with varied success, sought ways to sustain their operations by becoming less linear structurally and more diverse geographically. Among the most significant of these, in addition to IS, are Al Qaeda, Boko Haram, Al Shabaab, and Hezbollah.

Al Qaeda

IS made its presence felt dramatically when it seized Mosul, Iraq's second largest city, in summer 2014. But if a "terrorism era" is underway, most in the West would associate its beginning with the rise of Al Qaeda during the 1990s, and particularly with Al Qaeda's "9/11" attacks on the United States in 2001. (Details about the rise of Al Qaeda and Osama bin Laden are to be found in Lawrence Wright's superb book, *The Looming Tower.*) While bin Laden was on the run and then after his death in 2011, Al Qaeda's structure changed from that of a traditional top-down, pyramid-type organization to more of a network, with several Al Qaeda franchises spun off from Al Qaeda's central command. These include Al Qaeda in the Islamic Maghreb (AQIM), Al Qaeda in the Arabian Peninsula (AQAP), Al Qaeda in the Indian Subcontinent (AQIS), and Jabhat al-Nusra in Syria, all of which have operated with considerable autonomy even as they share the Al Qaeda brand.

That brand, however, can prove problematic. In July 2016, Jabhat al-Nusra changed its name to Jabhat Fateh al-Sham and declared itself separate from Al Qaeda, ostensibly to define itself to the public as solely a Syrian rebel force seeking the ouster of President Bashar al-Assad. To illustrate how convoluted terrorist politics can be, Ayman al-Zawahiri, Al Qaeda's chief, gave his blessing to the name change, saying that the group's ideology had not shifted. And yet another twist: Some Gulf states seeking Assad's removal reportedly promised the Nusra leaders that they would provide financial support to the group if it publicly broke with Al Qaeda.[3] Of course, all this did nothing to moderate the group's viciousness.

Recently, the most visible of the Al Qaeda affiliates has been AQAP, which has been an active force in the Yemen war and has sought to define some territory in Yemen as its own version of an "Islamic emirate." In this emirate, reported Robert Worth, "[T]he group rebuilt water, sewage, and electrical lines, and sought to increase the staffing of schools and hospitals. Al Qaeda also developed a media campaign to advertise its achievements."[4]

Meanwhile, bin Laden's successor, Ayman al-Zawahiri, who is hiding somewhere, occasionally issues edicts, to uncertain effect. Post bin Laden, Al Qaeda has become decentralized, which well suits its franchisees that want to share in a recognizable identity while defining their own courses of action in their respective locales.

Although IS's parent was one of these franchises, Al Qaeda in Iraq, Al Qaeda has been eclipsed by IS partly because Al Qaeda promised a caliphate at an undetermined time in the future, after successful war against near and far enemies (apostate states in the Arab world and the infidel West). But IS didn't wait; it declared its caliphate during the early stages of its war within Iraq and Syria, and its

---

[3] Mariam Karouny, "Syria's Nusra Front May Leave Al Qaeda to Form New Entity," *Reuters*, March 4, 2015, http://uk.reuters.com/article/uk-mideast-crisis-nusra-insight-idUKKBN0M00G620150304 [accessed October 3, 2015].

[4] Worth, *A Rage for Order*, 173.

success in taking and holding territory gave it credibility. In doing so, it claimed that the boundaries imposed by the 1916 Sykes-Picot Agreement, which divided the Middle East among the victorious powers in World War I, were null and void. Further, attention-getting attacks in France, the United States, Belgium, and elsewhere (including numerous bombings within Iraq) were IS organized or inspired, while Al Qaeda's most significant activity occurred in Yemen, which attracted mostly just regional notice and responses.

Tensions between Al Qaeda and IS simmered. A 2014 British government report observed that Al Qaeda "has been engaged in a very public battle with the Islamic State of Iraq and the Levant. After disowning ISIL and declaring it to no longer be an AQ affiliate. AQ has suffered the embarrassment of seeing the ISIL brand growing in strength whilst, at the same time, its own standing in the global *jihad* has taken a nosedive." The report further noted that "AQ is an organization based on a long-term strategy: it has been undone by the pace of real-world events."[5]

Al Qaeda should not, however, be dismissed as an impotent dinosaur. Consider its presence in the Indian subcontinent, where tensions are always high between Muslims and Hindus and between Pakistan and India. The religious-political situation there provides opportunities for creating horrific turmoil, as Pakistani and Indian counterterrorism officials well know. Further, while IS sustains major losses of its territory and fighters, Al Qaeda remains more elusive and more intact, even if maintaining a lower profile in much of the world's field of vision.

Al Qaeda is not on the run. In what might prove to be a wise strategic move, it has intensified its activity in western Africa while Syria and Iraq command most of the counterterrorism world's

<hr>

[5] Foreign and Commonwealth Office, "Al Qaida versus ISIL: The Battle for Ownership of the Global Jihad," November 2014, www.gov.uk/government/uploads/system/uploads/attachment_data/file/415547/FINAL_AQ_v_ISIL.pdf [accessed February 3, 2015].

attention. During the first half of 2016, Al Qaeda in the Islamic Maghreb (AQIM) and its localized subsidiaries launched more than 100 attacks in Mali and in neighboring countries, despite the presence of French troops and UN peacekeepers. Since 2013, more than eighty of the peacekeepers and six other UN employees have been killed in Mali, making it the world's most dangerous UN peacekeeping assignment.[6]

The Mali case is instructive; it might well prove to be a prototype for further Al Qaeda activity. Mali's military and financial limitations are such that the country's government absolutely must have outside assistance to address the Al Qaeda threat. AQIM has been able to count on outsiders of its own – Arab fighters who gained combat experience in Libya and elsewhere – and it was linked to the attack on the US consulate in Benghazi, Libya in 2012 during which US Ambassador Christopher Stevens and three other Americans were killed. Further, a significant number of immigrants from Mali (and from Mauritania and Senegal) live in France, perhaps providing a haven for extremists from their homeland. This is also an issue for the United States, wrote Yochi Dreazan: "Africa's Islamists are able to take advantage of the fact that many of the continent's countries have porous borders; weak and corrupt central governments; undertrained and underequipped militaries; flourishing drug trades that provide a steady source of income; and vast, lawless spaces that are so large – and so far away from major American military bases like those in the Middle East and Afghanistan – that it would be difficult for the U.S. to mount effective counterterrorism efforts."[7]

---

[6] Caleb Weiss, "Al Qaeda Has Launched More Than 100 Attacks in West Africa in 2016," *Long War Journal*, June 8, 2016, www.longwarjournal.org/archives/2016/06/over-100-al-qaeda-attacks-in-west-africa-since-beginning-of-the-year.php [accessed July 12, 2016].

[7] Yochi Dreazan, "The New Terrorist Training Ground," *Atlantic*, October 2013, 62–3.

Mali also offers an illustration of how the scope of terrorist operations puts great pressure on counterterrorism strategists. The key to controlling extremist violence in Mali, at least for the foreseeable future, is the French military presence there. French troops have been more successful than indigenous forces in reducing the strength of AQIM and its supporters. But France's military leadership has had to increase the troop presence at home because of terrorist attacks there, and in Africa beyond Mali, where the fight against terrorist organizations in North Africa requires French participation.[8] Who can continue the fight the longest might prove to be the determining factor in the future of AQIM.

To Mali's east, a particularly vicious terrorist organization with ties to IS marauds through a large amount of territory in several countries.

Boko Haram

In terms of attracting attention through horrific acts, Boko Haram, roughly translated from Hausa as "Western education is forbidden," sometimes outdoes IS. The central African group is based in the Chad Basin area of northeastern Nigeria, spilling over into neighboring countries. It has declared allegiance to IS (the significance of this is mostly symbolic), and is perhaps most notorious for its kidnapping of 276 schoolgirls from Chibok, Nigeria, in 2014, which led to the highly publicized (if not particularly effective) "Bring Back Our Girls" online campaign. By some calculations, Boko Haram is even more deadly than IS. In 2014, according to the Global Terrorism Database, while IS was responsible for 6,073 deaths, Boko Haram killed 6,644, 77 percent of whom were private citizens, compared to 44 percent of the IS-inflicted fatalities. These deaths occurred during the 453 terror attacks by Boko Haram, compared with 1,071 launched by IS.

---

[8] Christopher Chivvis, "Mali's Persistent Jihadist Problem," *Cipher Brief*, January 12, 2017, www.thecipherbrief.com/article/africa/malis-persistent-jihadist-problem-1089?utm [accessed January 13, 2017].

This underscores how lethal Boko Haram is in its work.[9] One-time Boko Haram leader Abubakar Shekau declared, "I enjoy killing anyone that God commands me to kill, the way I enjoy killing chickens and rams."[10] Such bloodthirstiness, observed Alex Thurston, "antagonizes almost the entire spectrum of Muslims in its region," limiting its base to hard core jihadis.[11]

The South Africa–based research organization Africa Check has reported that Boko Haram operates with an umbrella-like structure, with its cells able to carry out attacks on their own. These cells, said an Africa Check report, recruit "foot soldiers as needed from an army of young men who are susceptible to extremist ideology and hope to benefit financially or otherwise." Financing for the group comes from kidnappings for ransom, bank robberies, and other criminal activity.[12]

As is the case in the propaganda war against IS, governments have claimed success in degrading Boko Haram's capabilities. But Boko Haram, like IS, has responded by expanding into new territory. In 2015, there were at least sixty-six Boko Haram attacks outside Nigeria, in Chad, Cameroon, and Niger, causing more than 1,400 deaths.

Meanwhile, some of the Nigerian government's efforts proved to be counterproductive. A team of Johns Hopkins University researchers reported, "The only way to defeat the group in the long run, besides organizing for effective counterinsurgency efforts, is

[9] Edward Delman, "The World's Deadliest Terrorist Organization," *Atlantic*, November 18, 2015, www.theatlantic.com/international/archive/2015/11/isis-boko-haram-terrorism/416673/ [accessed December 15, 2015].

[10] Helon Habila, *The Chibok Girls: The Boko Haram Kidnappings and Islamist Militancy in Nigeria* (New York: Columbia Global Reports, 2016), 24.

[11] Alex Thurston, *"The Disease Is Unbelief": Boko Haram's Religious and Political Worldview,"* Brookings Project on US Relations with the Islamic World, Analysis Paper No. 22, January 24, 2016, www.brookings.edu/wp-content/uploads/2016/07/Brookings-Analysis-Paper_Alex-Thurston_Final_Web.pdf [accessed August 8, 2016].

[12] Mike Smith, "Factsheet: Explaining Nigeria's Boko Haram and Its Violent Insurgency," Africa Check, September 22, 2014, https://africacheck.org/factsheets/factsheet-explaining-nigerias-boko-haram-and-its-violent-insurgency/ [accessed January 29, 2016].

for the government to move ahead with development efforts and initiatives for political accommodation. Central authorities continue to oversell their progress on the battlefield while underinvesting in measures to address northeastern Nigeria's abysmal poverty and marginality. They have also aggravated dissension through human rights abuses and repression. Without a more coherent political and developmental approach, declarations of victory will ring hollow and social disaffection will remain a salient threat to state legitimacy."[13]

That last observation about counterinsurgency methods is important as it relates to all terrorist organizations, not just Boko Haram. Overzealousness, particularly on the part of the military, can backfire and help to recruit new extremist fighters. Aside from the relatively small percentage of terrorist recruits who truly are psychopaths, many young men and women have been driven into extremist ranks by government brutality and corruption. This does not justify terrorism, but if counterterrorism measures are to have lasting effect, they must include political reform as well as military muscle. Combating Boko Haram, as is the case with all terrorist organizations, requires turning off the recruiting faucet as well as eliminating fighters on the battlefield.

Also at issue is the relationship between terrorism and insurgency. Traditionally, the two could be distinguished by pointing to the baseline definition of insurgency used by the US military: "an organized movement aimed at the overthrow of a constituted government through the use of subversion and armed conflict."[14] Terrorism can enter the picture in several ways: through the nature of tactics employed by the insurgents, as is the case with Boko Haram: "activities, such as suicide attacks, that may have little military value but

---

13 Hilary Matfess, Peter M. Lewis, and Nathaniel D. F. Allen, "Unbroken Boko Haram," *Foreign Affairs*, March 21, 2016, www.foreignaffairs.com/print/1117023 [accessed April 12, 2016].

14 *The U.S. Army-Marine Corps Counterinsurgency Field Manual* (Chicago: University of Chicago, 2007), 2.

create fear and uncertainty within the populace and government institutions."[15] Also, the use of terroristic measures far afield – as has been done by Al Qaeda, IS, and others – transcends traditional insurgency.

An insurgency may be considered legitimate – the American Revolution comes to mind. But as a practical matter today, in cases such as that of Boko Haram the efforts to overthrow a government are so imbued with terroristic behavior that any distinction that might place an insurgency on higher moral ground is pointless and misleading. Boko Haram may want to portray its operations as an insurgency based on its goal of overthrowing "a constituted government" in contested territory, but targeting civilians and relying on terror to intimidate local populations to achieve its purposes brings it within the definition of terrorism.

Whatever the conflict in Nigeria is called, large numbers of noncombatants suffer. Even beyond the highly publicized kidnapping of schoolgirls, women and children bear the brunt of Boko Haram's destructiveness. Visiting a displaced persons camp in northern Nigeria, Helon Habila found "mostly women walking about, children in tow. Most of the children did not belong to the women; they were orphans, abducted from their homes by Boko Haram or found wandering after the terrorists had killed their parents."[16]

The fight between Boko Haram and government forces meant that by late 2016 in the northeastern Nigerian state of Borno, three seasons had passed without a harvest; the only things planted in farmers' fields were landmines. The United Nations estimated that in 2016 nearly a quarter million children in Borno were suffering from severe acute malnutrition, and that 130 would die each day unless food reached them.[17] Inflicting such misery is yet another element of spreading terror.

[15] Ibid., 5.
[16] Habila, *The Chibok Girls*, 85.
[17] "Hunger Games," *Economist*, September 3, 2016, 41.

Al-Shabaab

Al-Shabaab ("the youth") has benefited from the chaos that for so long has plagued Somalia, where its initial goal was to establish an Islamist emirate linked to Al Qaeda. Senior al-Shabaab fighters gained combat experience with Osama bin Laden in Afghanistan and later fighting Ethiopian troops that have periodically intervened in Somalia. Al-Shabaab has also operated outside the country, embarking on high-profile terror operations in Uganda, Kenya, and elsewhere.

Beginning in 2010, al-Shabaab has displayed a sophisticated reliance on using media to reach external audiences and in its operations. In July 2010, the organization released a twenty-one-minute online "news" video titled "Mogadishu: The Crusader's Graveyard." With slick production values and a fluent English narration (plus Somali and Arabic subtitles), the video depicted al-Shabaab's claimed success against troops deployed by African Union Mission in Somalia (AMISOM). The video was apparently designed to appeal to possible recruits around the world; it referred to AMISOM as an "American-led Western cause," which is terminology designed to stir the interest of prospective jihadists. The video also targeted publics in Uganda and Burundi, warning them not to join the "African Crusaders." Along these lines, the program told Western governments that their support of AMISOM was futile.[18]

The Mogadishu video appeared when terrorist organizations were beginning to expand their online capabilities. At around the same time, Al Qaeda in the Arabian Peninsula published the first edition of its online English language magazine. All such efforts were two-pronged propaganda efforts – competitions among terrorist organizations to expand their notoriety among governments and publics, and to appeal to potential recruits. For al-Shabaab, this appeal was

---

[18] "Al-Shabaab's First News Video," *Critical Threats*, August 5, 2010, www.criticalthreats.org/print/1641 [accessed March 4, 2015].

directed especially to members of the Somali diaspora, offering a vivid display of its ferocity in the name of Islamic purity.

Al-Shabaab had first experimented with online messaging to external audiences as early as 2007, when it was still shoring up its support within its fractured homeland and establishing itself as a player within the global community of terrorist organizations. In addition to circulating news bulletins about its activity on jihadist networks, al-Shabaab created its own web pages, commemorating "martyrs" killed in its operations.[19]

Perhaps the most infamous of these operations was the 2013 attack on Nairobi's Westgate Mall, during which seventy-one people (including four of the attackers) were killed and more than 200 wounded. During the battle for the mall between al-Shabaab and Kenyan police and military, al-Shabaab kept up a steady stream of tweeted updates about the violence, some of which were countered by tweets from police. One of the latter urged "all Kenyans to ignore the propaganda of those intent on dividing us and breaking us down." Al-Shabaab's tweets in Somali and English had different content, with the former targeting a domestic audience and the latter a global one.[20]

This occasion illustrated the use of Twitter as an alternative news source – what al-Shabaab called "insurgent journalism." Al-Shabaab was attempting to offset mainstream news coverage that, of course, condemned the attackers. Al-Shabaab tried to counter this by claiming that the attack was legitimate retaliation for Kenyan military incursions into Somali territory.[21]

Al-Shabaab's approach to media in the Westgate case and at other times underscores how important it and other terrorist

---

[19] Stig Jarle Hansen, *Al-Shabaab in Somalia* (New York: Oxford, 2013), 59–67.

[20] "Al-Shabab Showed Gruesome Social Media Savvy during Attack," *CBS News*, September 24, 2013, www.cbsnews.com/news/al-shabab-showed-gruesome-social-media-savvy-during-attack/ [accessed September 27, 2013].

[21] Christopher Anzalone, "The Nairobi Attack and Al-Shabab's Media Strategy," *CTC Sentinel* (Combating Terrorism Center at West Point), October 24, 2013, www.ctc.usma.edu/posts/the-nairobi-attack-and-al-shababs-media-strategy [accessed November 3, 2013].

organizations consider the constant flow of news on the Internet and the opportunity that online venues offer for presenting views that mainstream news media will ignore or depict critically. Terrorist organizations know that there are many audiences for news, some of which might be eager to hear from the al-Shabaabs of the world. Those are the audiences among which the terrorist organizations' messages resonate and from which recruits come. It is hard to imagine any terrorist group today not having a carefully planned media strategy. IS's approach to this is examined in Chapter 4.

Hezbollah

As one of the senior citizens of the terrorist world, Hezbollah (Party of God) offers a useful case study of how an extremist group, as it matures, can become integrated, to a degree, within a country's political structure.

Hezbollah began as a resistance force combating Israeli occupation of southern Lebanon in the early 1980s, and its military activities have continued since then, most recently in Syria on behalf of President Bashar al-Assad. A de facto extension of Iran's Revolutionary Guards, from which it has long received weapons and training, Hezbollah is seen by some as a champion of Shi'a Muslims amidst a mostly Sunni Arab world. This is partly a function of Lebanon's population, which is unique within today's Arab countries because of its mix of religions: 54 percent Muslim, half Sunni and half Shi'a; 40 percent Christian; 5 percent Druze. Hezbollah's leader, Hassan Nasrallah, is arguably the most powerful political figure in Lebanon, where power is scattered among numerous factions, and he is highly popular in much of the rest of the Arab world (particularly among Shia) as well, partly because of his fervent anti-Israeli and anti-Western rhetoric.

Hezbollah has been accused of terrorist activity since its founding; bombings of US military barracks and the US embassy in Lebanon; the Khobar Towers bombing in Saudi Arabia; airplane hijackings; and numerous plots against Israeli interests. These activities have not, however, prevented Hezbollah from becoming a significant part of Lebanese society. With funding from Iran, Hezbollah has provided healthcare, water delivery, vocational education, and other services.[22]

Lina Khatib wrote in 2012 that Hezbollah "is the leading Islamist group in the world in terms of possessing a sophisticated image management strategy" that relies on media outlets and products, public displays, and personified politics.[23] It has its own broadcasting station, Al Manar, which has expanded the Hezbollah constituency and brought the organization's voice to much of the Middle East, and to reach out even farther it features an English language news website, *alahednews*, and other venues in several languages.

Officially designated as a terrorist organization by the United States and other countries, Hezbollah stands out for its success not only in maintaining its military presence at home and abroad, but also being a political party that dispenses aid and patronage in ways not unlike the political machines in some Western countries. For terrorist organizations that want to establish themselves as permanent political fixtures, the Hezbollah model has considerable appeal.

Lessons from the histories of Al Qaeda, Boko Haram, Al Shabaab, Hezbollah, and other established groups are not lost on the leaders of IS. The people who direct terrorist organizations such as IS are not stupid. If they were, they and their followers would soon be dead. As committed political and religious ideologues, they understand the importance of their organizations being able to sustain a prolonged struggle and being nimble enough to meet changes in the political, religious, and financial dynamics affecting that struggle.

They further realize that their organization must be designed to survive the loss of members of its leadership cadre. If Osama bin Laden had been killed soon after the 9/11 attacks, Al Qaeda would have dealt with a far more damaging blow than happened when US

---

[22] Judith Palmer Harik, *Hezbollah: The Changing Face of Terrorism* (London: I. B. Tauris, 2004), 81–94.
[23] Lina Khatib, *Hizbullah's Image Management Strategy* (Los Angeles: Figueroa Press, 2012), 5.

forces killed him a decade later. By that time, the Al Qaeda franchises were operating effectively, with far less reliance on bin Laden. His removal was certainly useful, but it did not cripple Al Qaeda.

The IS leadership structured the caliphate in such a way that no one person would be indispensable to its survival. During early 2016, coalition forces reported that they had killed several top IS leaders. Heavy news coverage of these deaths might have been useful in discouraging potential IS recruits from joining the group, and as with any organization, the IS leadership pool was not limitless in its depth. But how much damage had been done to IS functionality depended on how well IS responsibilities had been dispersed and its back-up structure had been designed.

Although Abu Bakr al-Baghdadi is the best known leader of IS, much of the design and long-term planning for IS was reportedly overseen by Samir Abd Muhammad al-Khlifawi, also known as Haji Bakr. He had been a colonel in Iraq's air defense force intelligence service under Saddam Hussein, and had been cut adrift when the United States ordered the Iraqi military disbanded in 2003. After Haji Bakr was killed by anti-Assad rebels in northern Syria in 2014, a trove of documents was found in his home and made available to the German magazine *Spiegel*. Included were detailed blueprints for collecting intelligence about communities that IS would take over as part of its development, first in Syria and then in Iraq. Also among the documents were complex organizational charts to be used for setting up administrative structure. The precision and breadth of the plans are impressive and make clear that IS was carefully designed.[24]

As terrorist groups become more organizationally sophisticated, they will rely more on network theory in their design. Dispersed but still connected is the basic geography of networks, and networks' efficiency is enhanced by new communication technologies. The US

[24] Christoph Reuter, "Secret Files Reveal the Structure of Islamic State," *Spiegel Online*, April 18, 2015, www.spiegel.de/international/world/islamic-state-files-show-structure-of-islamist-terror-group-a-1029274.html [accessed May 11, 2015].

9/11 Commission labeled Al Qaeda a "stateless network,"[25] but it might be that Al Qaeda and other terrorist entities are evolving from stateless networks to networked states, which will make them even more dangerous and more difficult to subdue. Before the US invasion of Afghanistan in 2001, Al Qaeda featured both a hub-and-spoke structure, in which cells communicated directly with bin Laden and the organization's other leaders, and a wheel structure that allowed cells to communicate with one another without necessarily connecting with the leadership.[26] The network may become even looser, relying more heavily on media connections for its cohesion. Gabriel Weimann wrote that "the advantage of this operational structure is that surveillance, penetration, or capture of operatives does not lead the intelligence agency to other cells or to the central control structure."[27]

Al Qaeda also laid the foundation for intensive use of Internet-based media to extend its influence. On one of the websites it used, Al Qaeda displayed this message: "We strongly urge Muslim internet professionals to spread and disseminate news and information about the *Jihad* through e-mail lists, discussion groups, and their own websites. If you fail to do this and our site closes down before you have done this, we may hold you to account before Allah on the Day of Judgment."[28]

This is how a virtual state sustains itself. It uses new media technologies as its infrastructure, which allows organizational cohesiveness without the vulnerabilities of physical presence. Targeting a virtual entity solely in conventional ways is unlikely to be effective. Attack an online presence and poof – it's gone, only to pop up elsewhere.

---

[25] National Commission on Terrorist Attacks upon the United States, *The 9/11 Commission Report* (New York: W. W. Norton, 2004), 363.

[26] Michele Zanini and Sean J. A. Edwards, "The Networking of Terror in the Information Age," in John Arquila and David Ronfeldt (eds.), *Networks and Netwars* (Santa Monica, CA: RAND, 2001), 34.

[27] Gabriel Weimann, *Terror on the Internet* (Washington, DC: US Institute of Peace, 2006), 115.

[28] Ibid., 66.

IS, as a "state," has moved beyond this. It has a citizenry of sorts and engages in the mechanics of governance, as well as in military and terror operations. This means that dealing with IS is different from confronting previous terrorist organizations. Unlike a virtual state, it has territory and easily identified physical targets that can be attacked. IS has accepted this as the price of being able to offer a true jihadist homeland.

GOVERNING THE CALIPHATE

For a while, the model of the modern terrorist organization was Al Qaeda, with its increasingly sophisticated virtual structure and use of internal and external media. IS has taken a quantum leap beyond the Al Qaeda model, seizing cities such as Mosul in Iraq and Raqqa in Syria, and claiming territory estimated at one point in 2014 to be 81,000 square miles (roughly the size of Great Britain), although how much of that was truly *controlled* by IS was debatable.[29] (How much of Iraq or Syria was controlled by those countries' "real" central governments was also debatable.) By the end of 2015, IS was estimated to have lost 14 percent of the territory it had held in Iraq and Syria at the beginning of the year,[30] and by mid-2016 the loss was up to about 40 percent of what it had once proclaimed part of the caliphate. These numbers tend to be imprecise because when IS was forced to withdraw from one area, it would often appear in another, and "control" has flexible meaning.

---

[29] Rick Noack, "Here's How the Islamic State Compares with Real States," *Washington Post*, September 12, 2014, www.washingtonpost.com/news/ worldviews/wp/2014/09/12/heres-how-the-islamic-state-compares-to-real-states/ [accessed September 14, 2014]; Kathy Gilsinan, "The Many Ways to Map the Islamic 'State,'" *Atlantic*, August 27, 2014, www.theatlantic.com/international/ archive/2014/08/the-many-ways-to-map-the-islamic-state/379196/ [accessed September 20, 2014].

[30] Sergio Pecanha and Derek Watkins, "ISIS's Territory Shrank in Syria and Iraq This Year," *New York Times*, December 18, 2015, www.nytimes.com/interactive/2015/ 12/18/world/middleeast/Where-ISIS-Gained-and-Lost-Territory-Islamic-State.html [accessed December 19, 2015].

Administration

Whatever territory IS occupied was brought within the organization's governance structure. Part of this is a Shariah Council that oversees religious and judicial matters, such as observance of shariah law and "Islamic conduct," which includes wearing proper attire, not smoking, and praying five times daily. "Moral police" attend to such matters, while a regular police force handles traditional law enforcement. Courts are accessible to individual citizens who want to bring cases. This entire legal system is central to IS maintaining its authority. As Abdel Bari Atwan noted, "[O]nce a citizenry submits to the law of a government, it is accepting its authority and asking it to guarantee security."[31]

IS government also incorporates these agencies[32]:

- Security and Intelligence Council, led by veterans of Saddam Hussein's security service, which targets spies and dissidents.
- Military Council, which oversees defense and expansion of IS territory.
- Economic Council, which administers the IS taxation system, its oil revenues, and budgeting. In early 2015, it set the annual budget at US$2 billion.
- Education Council, which regulates curricula based on Salafist interpretation of the Qur'an. It has allowed girls to attend school and has established all-female schools.
- Islamic Services Council, which maintains infrastructure, such as roads, power, sanitation, and food distribution.
- Institution for Public Information, which produces IS propaganda, mostly online.

Just so we don't forget what we are dealing with, it is important to note that the IS government also includes offices for building improvised explosive devices and arranging transportation for suicide bombers. This is not Plato's republic.

---

[31] Abdel Bari Atwan, *Islamic State: The Digital Caliphate* (Oakland: University of California Press, 2015), 140.
[32] Ibid., 138–42.

The breadth and sophistication of the IS governance structure is significant regardless of the eventual fate of IS. It underscores the ways that the nature of terrorism continues to evolve, from individuals to rag-tag groups to quasistates. As complexity increases, so too does resilience. If IS had to face only the militaries of Iraq and Syria, unaided by major powers such as the United States and Russia, the battlefield outcome might be different. Even if IS is defeated in Iraq and Syria in a military sense, it will almost certainly continue to orchestrate terror attacks in Europe and elsewhere, and its structural residue is likely to be built upon by successors that might take the concept of a terrorist state to new levels of permanence.

A preview of the next stage of IS governance might have been on view during its period controlling the Libyan city of Sirte. Libya's post-Qaddafi chaos was inviting to IS, as were its oil and natural gas reserves that could strengthen the IS treasury. While IS prospects in Iraq and Syria were becoming increasingly problematic, North Africa appealed as both a haven and a new front for IS's holy war.

By early 2016, IS was establishing a government in this newest province, gradually modifying some of the administrative measures it had employed in Iraq and Syria. Sudarsan Raghavan reported that initially IS imposed strict shariah rule, which ranged from requiring stores to close during the daily prayer times, and extended to beheadings and other severe punishments for thieves, adulterers, and people caught drinking alcohol or smoking. These penalties were imposed by a court system that acquitted some defendants. Local officials who were in place when IS arrived could continue to serve once they pledged allegiance to their new boss. IS operated a radio station that broadcast Koranic verses and news about IS operations. They employed workers to keep the streets clean, and when IS fighters went into a shop, they paid for what they wanted. IS also recruited doctors, lawyers, and engineers from Libya and elsewhere (mostly North and sub-Saharan Africa and Saudi Arabia). IS administrators set up a system of licenses for shops and transactions such as selling a car.[33]

Backed by US air power, Libya's Government of National Accord drove IS out of Sirte at the end of 2016. The surviving IS fighters scattered, some slipping into Tunisia and others moving to other countries. Just as soldiers pick up new skills in every theater of combat, so too those responsible for administration develop more efficient practices each time they use them. The short-lived IS regime in Libya was exceedingly brutal, but seemed to pay greater attention to making the "province" run smoothly. Whether it will be IS or some new terrorist organization that next wants to build its own state or caliphate, it will almost certainly have learned from the IS experience during the period beginning in 2014, when IS was most forcefully on the march and establishing its version of governance.

Follow the Money

Terrorism requires money. Often, not much is needed; most of the materials for a bomb can be found in a pharmacy or hardware store. The planning and execution of the 9/11 attacks in the United States are estimated to have cost between US$400,000 and $500,000. This money was provided by Al Qaeda, which had pre-9/11 annual operating costs of about US$30 million, raised through donations.[34]

IS operates at an entirely different level and acquires its money differently than Al Qaeda did. As Jacob Shapiro observed, "While terrorism can be carried out on the cheap, holding territory is costly."[35] Rather than relying heavily on donors whose contributions might be traced and shut down by law enforcement agencies, IS uses the

---

[33] Sudarsan Raghavan, "Inside the Brutal but Bizarrely Bureaucratic World of the Islamic State in Libya," *Washington Post*, August 23, 2016.

[34] National Commission on Terrorist Attacks, *Report*, 169–70.

[35] Jacob Shapiro, "A Predictable Failure: The Political Economy of the Decline of the Islamic State," *CTC Sentinel*, Combating Terrorism Center at West Point 9 (94), www.ctc.usma.edu/posts/a-predictable-failure-the-political-economy-of-the-decline-of-the-islamic-state [accessed October 6, 2016].

resources of conquered territories.[36] It moves that money through a network of money exchange offices that transfer cash in and out of the areas under IS control.[37]

Estimates of the value of IS holdings vary greatly. Brett McGurk, the US Special Presidential Envoy of the Global Coalition to Counter ISIL, said in early 2016 that IS "was taking in about a billion dollars a year: five hundred million dollars in oil and gas and five hundred million in other forms of revenue – taxes, extortion, antiquities, kidnapping."[38]

Earlier appraisals of IS income were much higher. An October 2014 Thomson Reuters study found that IS had annual income of nearly US$3 billion, derived from more than US$2 trillion in assets that it controlled.[39] *The Economist* in December 2015 reported IS's GDP at US$6 billion. As for cash, IS scavenged successfully. When it attacked Mosul in 2014, IS seized more than US$425 million from one bank vault there. As it expanded, IS even created a handbook for its financial operations, *Principles of Administration.*[40]

As intriguing as all the numbers may be, it is important to keep in mind that no outsider really *knows* the state of IS finances. Like the combat situation, the IS economy was faring well when it was opposed almost solely by the Iraqi and Syrian governments. But when the United States, Russia, and others brought their air power into action, the vulnerability of key IS resources – principally the oil fields – quickly became apparent. Using a model based on other states' economic structures, Jacob Shapiro determined that it possessed

---

[36] Matthew Rosenberg, Nicholas Kulish, and Steven Lee Myers, "Predatory Islamic State Wrings Money from Those It Rules," *New York Times*, November 29, 2015.

[37] Margaret Coker, "How Islamic State's Secret Banking Network Prospers," *Wall Street Journal*, February 24, 2016.

[38] Robin Wright, "Is the Islamic State Hurting? The President's Point Man on ISIS Speaks Out," *New Yorker*, March 3, 2016, www.newyorker.com/news/news-desk/is-the-islamic-state-hurting-the-presidents-point-man-on-isis-speaks-out [accessed March 4, 2016].

[39] Jean-Charles Brisard and Damien Martinez, "Islamic State: The Economy-Based Terrorist Funding," Thomson Reuters, 3, https://risk.thomsonreuters.com/sites/default/files/GRC01815.pdf [accessed July 20, 2016].

[40] "Degraded, Not Yet Destroyed," *Economist*, December 12, 2015, 47.

neither revenue-generating nor administrative systems necessary to sustain itself, although he noted that, at least for the short term, IS was probably brutal and resilient enough to avoid collapse.[41]

Taxation and extortion (sometimes in the caliphate the two are indistinguishable) are pervasive, with taxes levied on telecommunication companies, trucks entering IS territory, and various small transactions. Those who want to loot archeological sites may do so, if they pay a tax on the value of what they steal. Non-Muslim communities must pay a protection tax.[42] Small-scale revenue-producing operations were also launched, such as creating a fruit and vegetable market in Mosul where vendors paid IS the equivalent of US$2,500 a year for a stall.

Oil provides the foundation for the caliphate's finances. Writing in 2015, Abdel Bari Atwan stated that IS was extracting 50,000 barrels of oil per day in Syria and 30,000 more in Iraq. By selling below market price, IS could find buyers and move its product, taking in as much as US$5 million a day. IS has also had gas fields and pipelines under its control. In addition to taxing looters of archeological sites, IS on its own stole antiquities, netting US$36 million from sales of these items from just one Syrian province. IS also sells people, primarily women as sex slaves.[43] Kidnapping is lucrative as well, generating millions of dollars each month in ransom payments.

Again, the variance in the published numbers about IS finances is important. It is due to two main factors. First, these are all estimates; IS does not open its books to the curious. Second, income and costs fluctuate according to the status of the conflict. When anti-IS air strikes destroy a bank holding IS cash or wipe out a large convoy of IS oil trucks, IS losses are so great that they cannot be made up by their remaining sources of income. Also, fighters must be paid, and the foreign recruits with previous military experience command premium salaries. Further, the amount of territory and number of

[41] Shapiro, "A Predictable Failure."
[42] Brisard and Martinez, "Islamic State," 5.
[43] Atwan, *Islamic State*, 147–8.

people under IS control change depending on the state of the war. At one point, IS controlled territory with nearly 10 million residents. As that number grows or shrinks, IS tax revenues do the same.[44]

For those outside the upper echelons of IS, guesswork is often the best available means of judging the caliphate's economic health. On any given day, air strikes might knock out a valuable IS oil convoy, or IS might seize some new territory, with financial loss or gain realized accordingly. As this is written, IS has apparently been dislodged from Libya, but if there is a turnaround – always possible given Libya's continuing turmoil – or if IS secures oil- and gas-rich territory elsewhere, its finances may recover.

Meanwhile, those seeking to destroy IS must understand that IS funding does not come just from the combat zone. As is described in Chapter 4, IS has proved skillful at using its knowledge of social media for fundraising as well as other purposes.

Women

IS has highlighted the role of women in building and sustaining the caliphate. In the world of terrorist organizations, this is unusual; women are rarely cited as contributors to an organization's work and often go unmentioned altogether. But in keeping with its plans for the long term, IS recruits women to become mothers of the next generation of fighters and to bring normalizing domesticity to the caliphate.

"Domesticity" in the caliphate presumably is different than that in other places, but a Quilliam Foundation analysis of IS proselytizing directed to women found the following elements of the IS case:

- By living in the caliphate and marrying fighters, women can free themselves from a life of *kufr*, disbelief.
- Women within the IS are part of a tightly knit sisterhood that provides friendship and support.

[44] Colum Lynch and David Francis, "The Billion-Dollar Caliphate," *Foreign Policy*, December 15, 2015, http://foreignpolicy.com/2015/12/15/the-billion-dollar-caliphate/ [accessed December 18, 2015].

- Providing a new generation of fighters is a crucial state-building role in the caliphate.[45]

Part of the IS bureaucracy is the all-female Al-Khanssaa Brigade, based primarily in Mosul and Raqqa. Al-Khanssaa is an activist group within IS, not mainly a fighting force, and it polices women to ensure appropriate religious behavior. It plays a significant role in recruiting women to the IS ranks, targeting Saudi Arabia and other Gulf states. As part of this effort, in early 2015 Al-Khanssaa issued "Women of the Islamic State." Charlie Winter, who translated and analyzed the document, found it to reflect the misogyny that underlies IS attitudes toward women. The manifesto makes clear that the role of women is "divinely" limited. Winter noted that the document was crafted for an audience of only Arab women; unlike many IS recruitment materials, this one was not translated into English or other languages. This was perhaps because women living in the West who might find the IS cause appealing are accustomed to more progressive attitudes about women's roles and may crave adventure and excitement rather than the "sedentariness, stillness, and stability" that this document touts.

Winter observed that the manifesto begins with a rebuttal of standards of Western civilization and then makes clear that women should aspire to nothing other than being mothers and homemakers. The exceptions: if they are studying theology, teaching or providing medical care to other women, or, in times of great danger, being ordered to fight to defend the Muslim community. The basic message about women's principal role is stated near the manifesto's conclusion: "May your sons be the bricks and mortar in the tower of majesty and minarets of the State of Islam."[46]

---

[45] Haras Rafiq and Nikita Malik, *Caliphettes: Women and the Appeal of the Islamic State* (London: Quilliam Foundation, 2015), 8–9, www.quilliamfoundation.org/wp/wp-content/uploads/publications/free/caliphettes-women-and-the-appeal-of-is.pdf [accessed January 30, 2016].

[46] Charlie Winter (trans.), *Women of the Islamic State* (London: Quilliam Foundation, 2015), 5–9, 41, www.quilliamfoundation.org/wp/wp-content/uploads/publications/free/women-of-the-islamic-state3.pdf [accessed February 2, 2016].

That manifesto describes glowing prospects for *Muslim* women. If a woman is not Muslim and she falls into the hands of IS, her life may become horrific. In 2014, when IS captured Mount Sinjar, near Mosul, they seized thousands of Yazidis, members of a pre-Islamic, Mesopotamian religious community. Yazidi women were treated as sex slaves. This occurred not in the random fashion of individual fighters considering women to be spoils of war, but rather as an organized market that had been designed in advance to facilitate rape on a large scale. IS said this was supported by the Qur'an (much the way some people justified American slavery as being sanctioned by the Bible), but Islamic theologians take issue with this.[47]

Setting theology aside, the experience of the Yazidis illustrates the IS attitude toward women more generally. They are chattels to be used, nothing more. Their victimization deserves more attention. It is evidence of the criminality that runs through the IS quasistate. The only thing that may be worse than the IS treatment of women is its manipulation of children.

Children

IS, Al Shabaab, Boko Haram, and other terrorist groups have in common their view that children are most useful as cannon fodder. Between January 2015 and January 2016, IS propaganda eulogized eighty-nine children and youth as martyrs. Of these, nearly half died when they detonated vehicle-borne improvised explosive devices and almost as many died as foot soldiers in battlefield operations.[48]

Further, IS videos have featured children executing prisoners or otherwise participating in violence. This reflects the milieu in which children within the IS caliphate are being raised. Surrounded by violence and the accompanying IS propaganda from their earliest years,

---

[47] Rukmini Callimachi, "ISIS Enshrines a Theology of Rape," *New York Times*, August 14, 2015.

[48] Mia Bloom, John Horgan, and Charlie Winter, "Depictions of Children and Youth in the Islamic State's Martyrdom Propaganda 2015–2016," *CTC Sentinel*, February 18, 2016, www.ctc.usma.edu/posts/depictions-of-children-and-youth-in-the-islamic-states-martyrdom-propaganda-2015–2016 [accessed March 10, 2016].

these children will not need to be converted to radicalism; they are born into it. The numbers are substantial and growing; in addition to the sons of IS fighters, orphans, and children who are kidnapped, in early 2016, according to one intelligence official's estimate, there were 31,000 pregnant women in the caliphate.[49] If IS remains in control, many of these women's children will be destined for IS ranks.

Borrowing a term from Saddam Hussein's regime, IS refers to its child-fighters as "Lion Cubs." They are sent on suicide missions, required to give their blood to wounded fighters, and are expected to report "traitors." Their socialization into IS life begins when the boys are very young; they are given sweets and hold IS flags. Then, when they are enrolled in IS schools, spotters select those they think ready for training, which includes being beaten (to "toughen" them) and practicing beheadings on "infidel" dolls. From there, it is on to the battlefield.[50]

Terrorist organizations' ruthless use of children is even more pronounced in attacks launched by Boko Haram. Since 2014, according to the United Nations, 20 percent of all of Boko Haram's suicide bombings have been carried out by children. The number of children involved in these attacks rose from four in 2014 to forty-four in 2015.[51] Some of these juvenile Boko Haram bombers are reported to be girls from the highly publicized kidnapping of schoolgirls in Chibok, Nigeria, in April 2014, as well as from other mass kidnappings by Boko Haram.[52]

[49] Noman Benotman and Nikita Malik, *The Children of Islamic State* (London: Quilliam Foundation, 2016), 8, www.quilliamfoundation.org/wp/wp-content/uploads/publications/free/the-children-of-islamic-state.pdf [accessed June 11, 2016].

[50] Katrin Kuntz, "Islamic State's Child Soldiers: First Come the Sweets, Then the Beheadings," *Spiegel Online*, July 29, 2016, www.spiegel.de/international/world/islamic-state-how-the-is-trains-child-soldiers-a-1103941.html [accessed August 15, 2016].

[51] Kevin Sieff, "Boko Haram Is Forcing More Children to Carry Out Suicide Bombings," *Washington Post*, April 12, 2016.

[52] Alexis Okeowo, "Two Years after the Nigerian Girls Were Taken," *New Yorker*, April 13, 2016, www.newyorker.com/news/daily-comment/two-years-after-the-nigerian-girls-were-taken [accessed April 20, 2016].

Women and girls captured by Boko Haram are trained in suicide bombing and beheading. ("When severing heads, cut from behind; they die faster," they are told.) After being taught what purportedly are lessons from the Qur'an, the girls are told that a suicide mission offers a direct path to heaven. Boko Haram has increased its use of women and girls in such attacks partly because they will rarely be searched thoroughly by male soldiers they may encounter.[53]

Meanwhile, Al Shabaab has "recruited" (usually meaning kidnapped) children as young as fourteen to join the ranks of its fighters. Despite condemnation from much of the world of the use of child soldiers, Al Shabaab continues to deploy them in its attacks.

New Fighters

Not everyone who joins the ranks of terrorist groups' fighters is compelled to do so. The flow of foreign fighters into IS territory depends partly on the state of combat and media depictions of IS's prospects, as well as IS's own recruiting. During the past several years, roughly 30,000 foreign fighters came to the caliphate, and when they arrived they had to complete paperwork, because even terrorist caliphates like their bureaucracies. Thousands of forms the incoming fighters completed fell into the hands of news organizations; a collection of about 4,600 documents produced between early 2013 and late 2014 were examined by NBC News and passed on to the Combating Terrorism Center (CTC) at West Point, where they were carefully analyzed. Among the CTC findings:[54]

- The fighters came from seventy countries. Saudi Arabia and Tunisia supplied by far the biggest numbers.

---

[53] Dionne Searcy, "Boko Haram Turns Female Captives into Terrorists," *New York Times*, April 8, 2016.

[54] Brian Dodwell, Daniel Milton, and Don Rassler, *The Caliphate's Global Workforce: An Inside Look at the Islamic State's Foreign Fighter Paper Trail*, Combating Terrorism Center at West Point, US Military Academy, April 2016, www.ctc.usma.edu/v2/wp-content/uploads/2016/06/Caliphates-Global-Workforce1.pdf [accessed May 3, 2016].

- The fighters were relatively well educated, with the largest contingent having high school education and the second largest having attended college.
- The unemployment rate of the fighters was generally no greater than the overall rate in their home countries. The most populated IS job categories were lower-skilled positions, which when considered along with the relatively higher educational levels may indicate that some fighters might have become frustrated by being unable to find work that matched their skills.
- About 10 percent of the fighters reported having previous jihadist experience, primarily in Syria, Libya, and Afghanistan. A significant number of these recruits had left Al Qaeda–affiliate Jabhat al-Nusra to come to IS.
- The recruits were asked to check their job preference: fighter, suicide bomber, or suicide fighter (someone who engages in a combat that he is unlikely to survive). Only 12 percent selected a suicide role.
- When asked their level of knowledge of shariah, 70 percent responded "basic," 23 percent "intermediate," and 5 percent "advanced." Those selecting "advanced" were least likely to choose a suicide combat role.

When you watch videos showing IS fighters in action, whether in regular combat, committing atrocities, or even just enjoying some time away from their war, you may wonder, "Just who are these guys?" These data provided the beginning of some answers.

Interrogation and sometimes press interviews also help with understanding who the fighters are and how the IS operates. An IS volunteer from Germany, Harry Sarfo, was arrested when he returned home and he talked extensively with security officials and with the *New York Times*. He said that his time in Syria had been cut short because he, like numerous other European recruits, was told that he was more needed to carry out attacks in his homeland. He added that he learned that IS had a special directorate for intelligence and external operations, directed by one of the most senior IS leaders, Abu Muhammad al-Adnani (who was later killed by a US airstrike). Further, Sarfo said he was told that IS was shorthanded in Germany and Britain, but had plenty of operatives in France. As for the United States, sending volunteers back into America was difficult, but because guns were so easily available (not requiring an IS person to acquire and deliver them), social media were adequate for finding prospective attackers. Sarfo stated that foreign fighters were told to make their trip to the region look like they were going on a holiday in Turkey, booking roundtrip tickets and making reservations at a Turkish hotel. Once in Turkey, they were smuggled into Syria, given a few days of training, and then sent back into Turkey and on to home.[55]

Sarfo's story was convincing, and it provided interesting insights about IS operations. He told journalists and German authorities that he had not participated in any violence, and he received only a short prison sentence when he returned to Germany. But after a video surfaced showing him participating in an IS execution of prisoners in Syria, Germany charged him with murder and war crimes.[56]

Any information coming from sources within IS is likely to be self-serving, as Sarfo's story was. But intelligence services and other agencies need to build on whatever they can find to better understand IS and other terrorist organizations. All this information gathering should be infused with a sizable dose of skepticism as pieces of the puzzle are added and discarded.

THE TERRORIST UNIVERSE EXPANDS

When combating a major terrorist organization such as Al Qaeda, Boko Haram, or IS, governments' principal tools include kinetic force: air power and troops on the ground. This approach can be successful, but only up to a point. Strikes by missiles, aircraft, and drones can inflict considerable damage on people and objects. Without doubt, the air attacks conducted by the United States and others against

---

[55] Rukmini Callimichi, "How a Secretive Branch of ISIS Built a Global Network of Killers," *New York Times*, August 3, 2016.

[56] Greg Miller and Souad Mekhennet, "Militant Who Denounced Islamic State Faces Murder, War Crimes Charges in Germany," *Washington Post*, January 3, 2017.

IS in Syria and Iraq killed many IS fighters and destroyed valuable resources such as trucks used to carry oil and stockpiles of cash used to pay IS soldiers. Deploying troops in the fight means the chances of sustaining casualties are greater and thus less politically palatable. Also, the costs of military operations can be budget wreckers, forcing unpleasant decisions about priorities. Particularly after its experiences in Afghanistan beginning in 2001 and Iraq beginning in 2003, the United States has been wary of putting large numbers of "boots on the ground." The preference has been for quick, in-and-out special operations teams such as the Seal Team Six unit that killed Osama bin Laden, and other small squads that have killed or captured IS leaders.

As successful as such individual missions might be, they are ultimately unsuited for defeating terrorist organizations. Like a creature from a horror movie, a group such as IS can ooze its way across borders and reconstitute itself thousands of miles away from where it is supposedly being defeated. As IS was being pushed back from some of its territorial gains in Iraq and Syria, it was building its strength in Libya, where it threatens Tunisia, Algeria, Morocco, and other African countries.

Part of the difficulty in truly "defeating" IS is found in the organization's tactical adroitness, but IS also benefits from political factors, especially the inadequacies of central governments. Governance in Syria is piecemeal at best, and this makes it difficult to argue that replacing IS in the territory it holds – especially if the replacement is the Assad regime – would improve daily life for the people living there. In Iraq, the religious tensions that shape politics stretch back more than a thousand years. Iraq is roughly two-thirds Shia and one-third Sunni. Today's Iraqi army is mostly Shia, and a survey conducted in early 2016 found that in Mosul – Iraq's second largest city, controlled by IS from 2014 until 2017 – 74 percent of Sunni respondents said they did not want to be liberated by the Iraqi army on its own. Further, 100 percent of the Sunni respondents said they do not want to be liberated by Shia militias or Kurdish Peshmerga troops. This is not out of loyalty to IS; surveys found that an overwhelming majority of Iraqi Sunnis oppose IS. But the sectarian divide in Iraq is so pronounced that the minority Sunnis fear that they will be mistreated by Shia troops and the Shia-dominated Iraqi central government. IS, meanwhile, benefits from this discord, raising the specter of Shia revenge if the government retakes territory now under IS control.[57]

The solution most likely to be supported by Iraqi Sunnis would be an international peacekeeping force, but as of this writing, there is no indication that other countries want to step into the Iraqi morass and provide troops for such an effort. Nor would the Iraqi government be amenable to hosting more foreign troops on its soil. As for any prospective peacekeepers, based on the recent US experiences, the fear of being trapped in Iraq indefinitely probably would override any altruistic instinct.

Somalia is even less stable than Iraq, and Al Shabaab takes full advantage of that. Although 22,000 troops have been deployed by AMISOM, which has cost more than US$1 billion, this military effort is not well coordinated and Al Shabaab continues to prove resilient. The terrorist group finances its operations by smuggling charcoal, sugar, and other commodities, and like IS, it taxes traffic and businesses in areas that it controls. Al Shabaab slithers regularly into Kenya and other neighboring states, and has shown itself capable of carrying out attacks outside its home territory, as was the case in its 2013 attack on the Westgate Shopping Mall in Nairobi.[58]

Al Shabaab has suffered from infighting as Al Qaeda and IS seek its affiliation with them. Some Al Shabaab commanders picked one or the other, and meanwhile the United States intensified its airstrikes against the group. But neither the Somali government nor

---

[57] Munqith al-Dagher and Karl Kaltenthaler, "Why Iraqis Living under the Islamic State Fear Their Liberators," *Washington Post*, April 11, 2016, www.washingtonpost.com/news/monkey-cage/wp/2016/04/11/why-iraqis-living-under-the-islamic-state-fear-their-liberators/ [accessed April 12, 2016].

[58] Vanda Felbab-Brown, "Why Are Efforts to Counter al-Shabaab Falling So Flat?," Brookings Institution, April 5, 2016, www.brookings.edu/blogs/order-from-chaos/posts/2016/04/05-counterterrorism-state-building-somalia-felbabbrown [accessed April 11, 2016].

AMISOM could take and hold enough territory to fatally damage Al Shabaab. Like other guerrilla groups dating back millennia, Al Shabaab emphasizes mobility and decides carefully if and when it wants to stand and fight.

As with Boko Haram in western Africa, Al Shabaab could destabilize significant parts of its region if it is allowed to flow wherever it chooses. Physically containing a terrorist organization is essential if it is to be susceptible to conventional attacks, but the terrorists are fully aware of this and rely heavily on invisible mobility. This enhances their chances for survival and enables them to establish outposts distant from their original homes.

As these cases indicate, terrorist organizations require one principal enabling circumstance if they are to be successful: weak governance that has alienated populations or left unprotected the territory where the terrorists operate. Antiterrorist military force might counteract this, but only for a while. When the troops leave, disorder and extremist groups return.

Skills in irregular warfare do not prevent terrorist organizations from being badly damaged by those who fight them, especially when their enemies' militaries possess sophisticated weaponry such as cruise missiles and armed drones. But if terrorist organizations are to be defeated, it not only requires success on the battlefield, but also needs the flow of new terrorist recruits to be cut off. That has been made exceptionally difficult because many terrorist organizations – most notably IS – have brought innovation and persistence to their use of social and other Internet-based media for recruitment, training, fundraising, and other essential tasks. These new media venues are the virtual battlefields on which the terrorism versus counterterrorism battle is being fiercely fought.

4   Media Weaponry

When terrorists attacked the airport and a metro station in Brussels in March 2016, it was uncertain at first who was behind the bombings. But within hours, the Amaq News Agency, IS's in-house news service, posted – in English – an IS claim of responsibility, and the news quickly spread, first through Telegram, the favorite social media platform of IS, and then news organizations around the world picked up and reported the claim.[1] As global news coverage spread, IS could bask in its version of glory.

Much of Amaq's content, which includes news releases and videos, is in Arabic, but when it wants to tout a major story, its policy is "English first." The IS core constituency matters less than does its worldwide media audience. As for news organizations' role as couriers for Amaq (and thus for IS), consider the appeal of reporting a crime story with information provided by the perpetrator. Irresistible, assuming you are willing to pay no attention to the ethical disaster of collaborating with evil.

In this case and others, IS proved that it understood the flow of news and how easy it is to manipulate coverage. When the IS news tide was ebbing and the prevailing reporting was about IS losing territory in Iraq and Syria, IS reversed the flow through its attacks in Europe. News headlines went from "IS in retreat" to "IS on the attack," which was precisely what IS wanted. As Charlie Winter observed, "the media is the arena within which the war of ideas is waged, where the group's relevance – and, ultimately, its ideational

---

[1] Charlie Winter, "ISIS Is Using the Media Against Itself," *Atlantic*, March 23, 2016, www.theatlantic.com/international/archive/2016/03/isis-propaganda-brussels/475002/ [accessed March 25, 2016].

longevity – can best be preserved and perhaps enhanced, even as it experiences territorial losses."[2]

Understanding modern terrorism is impossible without understanding the complex relationship between terrorists and media. The purpose of terrorism is to terrorize. Killing people is a means to that end, not necessarily an end in itself. During the September 11, 2001 attacks on the United States, nearly 3,000 persons were killed, while many millions were terrorized as television repeatedly showed the airplanes hitting the World Trade Center towers, the resulting fires, people falling to their deaths, and finally the towers collapsing. Individual psyches digested the day's events, images, and losses in individual ways; an estimated 422,000 New Yorkers suffered from varying degrees of posttraumatic stress disorder as a result of the attacks.[3] Furthermore, the 9/11 attacks put Americans on notice that terrorism was not confined to distant places. Vulnerability was demonstrated, leaving a lingering question: "What next?" If Al Qaeda's goal was to instill terror, the attack was a success.

The logic behind modern terrorism is often convoluted. Although the terrorists' usual goal is to force a policy change, such as the release of prisoners or removal of a foreign presence from particular territory, that will be achieved only rarely. After the 9/11 attacks, as could have been predicted, the United States responded with militarized fury, uprooting the Taliban government of Afghanistan and killing large numbers of Al Qaeda fighters before Osama bin Laden and his remaining troops fled into Pakistan. The presumed long-range goal of bin Laden's 9/11 plan was to draw the United States into a war that would cause America and its allies to bleed so severely that they would fully withdraw from Muslim lands. This would allow Al Qaeda to turn its efforts to removing "apostate" governments in the Middle East and replacing them with rulers who truly embraced Islamic shariah law. Instead, Al Qaeda lost its safe haven

---

[2] Ibid.

[3] "9/11 by the Numbers," *New York Magazine*, http://nymag.com/news/articles/wtc/1year/numbers.htm [accessed October 23, 2014].

and America became even more entangled with the Muslim world, at least for the foreseeable future.

Of course, the United States has also bled heavily, physically and financially, throughout the military aftermath of 9/11. The Afghanistan conflict became America's longest war, and the concurrent campaign in Iraq has proved disastrous in numerous ways.

That said, it leaves unanswered the big question about terror and prolonged conflict: How do terrorists "win"? Terror attacks communicate anger and determination. If persistent and damaging enough, they will – at least in theory – undermine public support for policies the terrorists want to see changed. But that doesn't necessarily happen. The eleven years of Palestinian suicide bombings in Israel (1994–2005) that killed more than 600 Israelis did not produce gains for the Palestinians, but rather resulted in intensified Israeli occupation tactics including targeted assassinations of militants, tighter occupation of Palestinian towns, and eventually an increased physical separation through creation of a 400-mile wall-and-fence barrier.[4]

Terrorism is not the great equalizer that some of its proponents assume it to be. Whether it was the United States versus Al Qaeda, Israel versus Palestinian extremists, Russia versus Chechen rebels, or other cases in which a militarily strong country was subjected to terror attacks, the terrorists and their backers paid a disproportionate price for what proved to be insignificant steps toward their goals.

Nevertheless, whatever the target of a terrorist mission – whether it is a city bus or New York's World Trade Center – terrorists still seem to believe that they can achieve their purpose through the ripple effects of fear produced by news of the event as delivered to broad publics by various media.

If the perpetrators seek only limited return on their investment in terror, they might succeed. A good example is the effect that news of terror attacks can have on tourism, which is a vital component of the fragile national economies of countries such as Egypt and

---

[4] "Palestinian Suicide Attacks," BBC News, January 29, 2007, http://news.bbc.co.uk/2/hi/middle_east/3256858.stm [accessed December 3, 2015].

Tunisia. Particularly when tourists are targeted by terrorists, news reports about these attacks can produce quick results in terms of canceled tourist visits. Those who are killed or injured in the attacks matter less to the terrorists than do the people (and their money) who stay away from the targeted country for an extended time. Terrorism can also deter foreign investment in a country, causing further economic damage.

Over the longer term, terrorism can create conditions based on fear that change the way we live. Consider what it was like to board a commercial airline flight twenty years ago compared to the often-excruciating process of doing so today.

An unspoken symbiotic relationship exists between terrorists and news media. The terrorists rely on news coverage of their acts to generate the terror they want to cause. For their part, some news organizations will spotlight horrific acts of terrorism because such coverage attracts and holds audiences. In 1985, British Prime Minister Margaret Thatcher called for starving terrorists "of the oxygen of publicity on which they depend." She suggested that while an airplane hijacking was in progress, the news media should "not say or show anything which could assist the terrorists' morale or their cause while the hijack lasted."[5]

In advancing that idea, Thatcher underestimated both the media savvy and cold-bloodedness of terrorist groups. If news media imposed a coverage blackout on a terrorist "event," the terrorists could escalate their level of criminality – such as by killing hostages – until the story grew in importance to the point at which news organizations would feel compelled to cover the event. And today, in the era of social media, conventional news organizations' coverage decisions are of limited relevance in getting information to global audiences. Imposing a "news blackout" is not feasible because so many alternative venues exist through which information may be

[5] Margaret Thatcher, "Speech to the American Bar Association," July 15, 1985, www.margaretthatcher.org/document/106096 [accessed November 18, 2015].

disseminated. Also, journalists are supposed to tell their audiences what is going on. Only on rare occasions (such as a kidnapping in which news reports might endanger the victim) is suppressing information considered legitimate.

Overall, sophisticated terrorist leaders understand the news media better than most news professionals understand terrorism. Add to this the proficiency of groups such as IS in using social media and other web-based tools to disseminate information on their own, and it becomes clear that terrorist organizations can at least hold their own on media battlegrounds.

THE NEW MEDIA ENVIRONMENT

To borrow Margaret Thatcher's term, the supply of oxygen that sustains terrorists has greatly expanded during the three decades since she issued her warning. Traditional news organizations were then effective gatekeepers, exercising some control over how much attention terrorists and their activities received, how they were portrayed, and how they were viewed by the public. Terrorists could not reach mass publics on their own. Today, an individual can post a video or tweet and have unbounded access to the rest of the online world, with the possibility of a message going viral and quickly reaching millions. The gatekeepers of the past are less and less relevant.

Post-9/11 Al Qaeda found this new media world congenial and adopted the Internet as the best medium for sending and receiving messages to scattered audiences.[6] The Al Neda web site, which Al Qaeda began using in early 2002, published analyses of the wars in Afghanistan and Iraq, commentary by friendly Islamic clerics about Al Qaeda operations, and explanations of how Al Qaeda's war aims would benefit Islam by undermining the power of the United States, Israel, and allegedly apostate governments of Muslim states. The content of Al Qaeda–related sites, wrote Michael Scheuer, "adds up to a tremendous contribution to what bin Laden always has said is

---

[6] Some of the following material is drawn from Philip Seib and Dana Janbek, *Global Terrorism and New Media* (London: Routledge, 2011).

his and Al Qaeda's first priority: the instigation to jihad of as many Muslims in as many locales as possible."[7]

Al Qaeda's Internet operations gradually became more sophisticated and secure. According to a 2004 report by the US Justice and Treasury departments, the traditional espionage communication technique of the "dead drop" was adapted for online use. Selected Al Qaeda members were given the same prearranged user name and password for an e-mail account such as at Hotmail.com. One person would write a message, but instead of sending it he saved it in the "draft" file and signed off. Then someone else could access the account, read the message, and either leave it for someone else to read or delete it. Because the message was never sent as an e-mail, the Internet service provider retained no copy of it, and no record of it traversing the Internet existed.[8]

While devising secure methods of communicating, Al Qaeda was also building an online library of training materials that would teach its readers how to make ricin poison, how to build a bomb from commercial chemicals, and other useful advice. The online magazine *Muaskar al-Battar* (Camp of the Sword) told potential recruits, "Oh, Mujahid brother, in order to join the great training camps you don't have to travel to other lands. Alone in your home or with a group of your brothers you too can begin to execute the training program." The Al Qaeda–affiliated Global Islamic Media Front, primarily serving sympathizers living in Europe, featured online videos showing how to plan a roadside assassination, fire a rocket-propelled grenade and a surface-to-air missile, blow up a car, take hostages, and employ other tactics.[9]

Such training efforts could reach many people quickly and avoid the dangers of recruits gathering at a mosque or other place where they might be observed. John Arquilla noted that Al Qaeda

[7] Michael Scheuer, *Imperial Hubris* (Dulles, VA: Brassey's, 2004), 79, 81.

[8] Douglas Frantz, Josh Meyer, and Richard B. Schmitt, "Cyberspace Gives Al Qaeda Refuge," *Los Angeles Times*, August 15, 2004.

[9] Steve Coll and Susan B. Glasser, "Terrorists Move Operations to Cyberspace," *Washington Post*, August 7, 2005.

appreciated that "both time and space have in many ways been conquered by the internet," and Bruce Hoffman commented that the Internet offered Al Qaeda a "virtual sanctuary" because it is "the ideal medium for terrorism today: anonymous but pervasive."[10]

As well as providing instruction, Al Qaeda's early online material urged its readers to rally to the cause. *Sawt al-Jihad* (Voice of Jihad), an online magazine that first appeared in 2004, touted the accomplishments of mujahedin. Its tone is illustrated by this excerpt from an October 2004 editorial: "Muslims! Go out to [fight] Jihad for the sake of Allah! Paradise has already flung open its gates and the virgins of paradise are already decked out in anticipation of their grooms – this is Allah's promise. Allah will not grant peace of mind to anyone who has a heart until he has gone out to fight against Allah's enemies, as he was commanded."[11]

While proselytizing in such ways, the online magazines also reminded their readers of the importance of cybersecurity. The online *Technical Mujahid Magazine* was begun in late 2006 to instruct its readers about electronic data security and other high-tech matters. While stressing the need for caution, Al Qaeda pressed its followers to make full use of the Internet: "We strongly urge Muslim internet professionals to spread and disseminate news and information about the Jihad through e-mail lists, discussion groups, and their own websites. If you fail to do this, and our site closes down before you have done this, we may hold you to account before Allah on the Day of Judgment ... We expect our website to be opened and closed continuously. Therefore we urgently recommend any Muslims that are interested in our material to copy all the articles from our site and disseminate them through their own websites, discussion boards, and e-mail lists. This is something that any Muslim can participate in

---

[10] Ibid.

[11] Gabriel Weimann, *Terror on the Internet* (Washington, DC: US Institute of Peace, 2006), 65, 67; "Al Qaeda Internet Magazine *Sawt al-Jihad* Calls to Intensify Fighting during Ramadan," *Jihad Watch*, www.jihadwatch.org/archives/003647 [accessed February 20, 2009].

easily, including sisters. This way, even if our sites are closed down, the material will live on, with the Grace of Allah."[12]

Al Qaeda also created its own media production operation, As Sahab (The Cloud), which functioned under tight security requirements. A video of bin Laden, Zawahiri, or other Al Qaeda spokespersons would be shot in a remote location, hand-carried to a place where it was safe to upload it to the Internet, and then sent to As Sahab's postproduction facility. There it could be edited and dressed up with graphics and subtitles. The final video product was then put on a memory stick, taken by a courier to an Internet café, and uploaded to various Al Qaeda–affiliated websites. The addresses of those sites were then published in Internet forums and chat rooms, and Al Qaeda followers copied and distributed the videos. This system began in 2005, when Al Qaeda stopped delivering videotapes directly to Al Jazeera and other news organizations, which would edit them as they chose, sometimes diminishing the intended impact of the material.[13] The gatekeepers were becoming unnecessary and were pushed aside.

As Sahab's importance and productivity increased. In 2005, it released sixteen videos. By 2007, the number had reached ninety-seven original productions. By 2009, As Sahab was distributing videos showing Americans under attack in Afghanistan, posting videos in Urdu, and presenting a documentary series, "The Protectors of the Sanctuary," with forty-minute tributes to Al Qaeda supporters who had been killed.[14] The best known of the As Sahab videos were those featuring bin Laden, who said that 90 percent of his efforts were carried out through the media.[15]

[12] Ibid.

[13] "As Sahab: Al Qaeda's Nebulous Media Branch," *Stratfor Daily Terrorism Brief*, September 8, 2006; Craig Whitlock, "Al Qaeda's Growing Online Offensive," *Washington Post*, June 24, 2008.

[14] Whitlock, "Al Qaeda's Growing Online Offensive"; "As Sahab Posts," CBS News Internet Terror Monitor, www.cbsnews.com/sections/monitor/main502684.shtml ?keyword=As+Sahab&tag=contentMain;contentBody [accessed July 18, 2009].

[15] Peter Bergen, "Al Qaeda at 20, Dead or Alive?," *Washington Post*, August 17, 2008.

Among the most notable Al Qaeda online activities were those of Al Qaeda in Iraq (AQI), a particularly aggressive Al Qaeda subsidiary that became the parent of IS. When Abu Musab al-Zarqawi was leading AQI (he was killed in June 2006 in a US bombing raid), he used the Internet more consistently than any other terrorist figure. His first known online project was "Heroes of Fallujah," a 2004 video that showed men planting a roadside bomb and then watching as it blew up an American armored personnel carrier. This kind of video was so popular that AQI created a "Top 20" compilation of the best (or most horrific) such combat footage, and instituted a contest for which photographer sympathizers would be awarded points depending on how close they moved to the incident they were filming and how brutal their images were. Another of the Zarqawi products was the online magazine *Zurwat al-Sanam* ("Tip of the Camel's Hump," meaning ideal Islamic practice). Zarqawi's "information wing" also produced "All Religion Will Be for Allah," a 2005 video that presented forty-six minutes of war footage and a tribute to suicide bombers. The distribution of this video showcased the terrorists' increasing media sophistication: It appeared on a specially designed web page with numerous links for people who wanted to watch it in different formats. There was a version for those with a high-speed Internet connection, a simpler version for those using a dial-up connection, an option to use Windows Media or RealPlayer, and a version that could be played on a mobile phone, which was an advanced concept in 2005.[16]

Zarqawi was also behind one of the most hideous early online videos. AQI kidnapped American businessman Nicholas Berg, and Zarqawi beheaded the captive on camera. The video of this murder was posted on the web on May 11, 2004 and within twenty-four hours it had been copied onto other sites and downloaded more than 500,000 times.[17] Soon the number of viewers was in the millions.

---

[16] Susan B. Glasser and Steve Coll, "The Web as Weapon," *Washington Post*, August 9, 2005.

[17] Nadya Labi, "Jihad 2.0," *Atlantic Monthly*, July–August 2006, 102.

This incident was an early indicator of the value of the Internet to terrorists. Mainstream news organizations would not show such graphic footage to the public, but the Internet provided a way for Zarqawi to avoid traditional media filters and deliver whatever images he wanted to a vast audience. Based on the number of downloads, Zarqawi correctly gauged the tastes of those in the public that he wanted to reach. This is a hard core audience, not a general one, and Zarqawi had apparently decided that he would play to his strength, connecting with those who approved of his methods, rather than soften his appeal to make it more acceptable to a wider audience. IS has carried this forward.

In 2005, Zarqawi's media team began presenting regular Internet news broadcasts that were billed as "the sole outlet for mujaheddin media."[18] In addition to the newscasts, Zarqawi's media operation regularly issued online news releases about AQI's "victories" and video clips showing snipers, suicide bombers, and roadside bombs targeted at Americans in Iraq. In 2004, such clips were compiled in an hour-long video titled "The Winds of Victory," which was disseminated through Zarqawi's media organization and other terrorist websites.[19]

At the top of the Al Qaeda hierarchy, Ayman al-Zawahiri watched Zarqawi with concern. Just how extreme and narrow did Al Qaeda want its constituency to be? Wouldn't the eventual caliphate need support of more than the violence lovers to whom Zarqawi was appealing? Zawahiri chastised Zarqawi in a letter that told him he was jeopardizing the "circles of support, assistance, and cooperation" essential for the expansion of Al Qaeda's influence.[20] Zawahiri also told Zarqawi: "I say to you that we are in a battle, and that more than half of this battle is taking place in the battlefield of the media. And that we are in a media battle in a race for the hearts and minds of [the

---

[18] Marc Lynch, "Al Qaeda's Media Strategies," *National Interest*, Spring 2006.

[19] Scott Shane, "Zarqawi Built Global Jihadist Network on Internet," *New York Times*, June 9, 2006.

[20] Atwan, *Islamic State*, 50.

ummah]." He went on to advise Zarqawi that killing captives with bullets was preferable over beheadings. That, he wrote, "would achieve that which is sought without exposing ourselves to questions and answering to doubts. We don't need this."[21]

Zawahiri's fastidiousness may at first seem odd from a man who had no problem with airplanes being flown into office buildings. But it may have reflected Zawahiri's recognition that through the "battlefield of media" a broad activist constituency could be mobilized, and that this required a breadth of approach that was somewhat less spectacular than the ones Al Qaeda had embraced in the past. Enlarging a constituency requires political judgment and compromise, a concept that Zarqawi would not embrace. His descendants in terror who work for IS have, however, learned the value of relying on different content and tone in their media messages, depending on whom they want to reach. Within the span of a decade, terrorist media took a significant step forward in terms of its sophistication.

As the community of users of social media grew and the number of available online venues expanded, videos and other Al Qaeda products were not merely viewed; they could also be discussed online by members of their audience. Zawahiri seemed to recognize that a kind of courtship was required to attract recruits from this audience; hence his warning to Zarqawi about relying so heavily on graphic images. Zawahiri's own messages remained relatively conventional: repeatedly calling for the overthrow of the Saudi regime and praising the "blessed raids" of 9/11 on the fifteenth anniversary of the attacks.[22]

Several years later, IS media producers showed that they, too, were sensitive to the need to match content to audience and so

---

[21] Joby Warrick, *Black Flags: The Rise of ISIS* (New York: Doubleday, 2015), 185.

[22] Thomas Joscelyn, "Al Qaeda Releases Three New Messages from Ayman al Zawahiri," *Long War Journal*, January 14, 2016, www.longwarjournal.org/archives/2016/01/al-qaeda-releases-3-new-messages-from-ayman-al-zawahiri.php [accessed January 20, 2016]; Rowan Scarborough, "Ayman al-Zawahiri, al Qaeda Leader: 9/11 Attack 'Blessed,'" *Washington Times*, September 9, 2016, www.washingtontimes.com/news/2016/sep/9/ayman-al-zawahiri-al-qaeda-leader-911-blessed/ [accessed September 10, 2016].

produced messages for a range of potential viewers – everyone from the committed fighter who cared only about battlefield martyrdom to the physician who wanted to provide health care to the caliphate's children.

THE MEDIA CALIPHATE

We live in the era of virtual states, entities that eschew physical definition in favor of relying on the tools of cyberspace to govern, to serve their citizens, and even to wage war. The concept is still young and is taking shape most notably in the virtual connectivity between homelands and diaspora and in "stateless states" such as Kurdistan. It is also a boon to terrorist organizations such as Al Qaeda, which operates with networked affiliates that are not physically contiguous but are virtually linked, and IS, which has built media-based connections to a scattered global constituency.

IS is a hybrid version of the virtual state, with its caliphate on Syrian and Iraqi territory and its provinces in countries extending from Nigeria to Afghanistan, plus looser affiliations elsewhere in the world. The relatively conventional governance of the Syria–Iraq region is described in Chapter 3. Its geographic boundaries there can be defined, although they fluctuate depending on the state of the war. Much of the cohesion of IS is attributable to its skillful use of new media, especially social media, to provide its adherents with shared information, to recruit and stay connected with new "citizens," wherever they may be, and to deliver its messages to the wider world.

But the virtual state is not impervious to attack. Although cyberspace may be difficult to regulate or otherwise control, the tools used in this realm are vulnerable, and so must be designed and operated with care. IS's techies are sophisticated, creating an array of new media baubles: smartphone apps, multilingual videos, a radio station (*Al Bayan*), music (jihadist chants), an online magazine (*Dabiq*), and even video games. It also has its news agency, *Amaq*, which it uses to send news releases with headings such as "Breaking News" and "Exclusive."

While IS had to contend with just the Syrian and Iraqi armies and rival extremist groups, it could place major emphasis on such matters. The intervention of Russian and Western military forces, however, changed the nature of the conflict. In Syria, the Assad regime was given new life. In Iraq, the shaky army was bolstered by foreign "advisors." And within the caliphate, airstrikes killed IS fighters and smashed parts of its infrastructure. While all this was happening, social media giants such as Twitter and YouTube became more aggressive in shutting down accounts and removing IS content faster than it could be restored.[23]

Twitter is a favorite of IS and other extremists partly because it is so easy to open accounts. Some IS activists have hundreds of Twitter accounts that they use concurrently, often creating new ones as quickly as Twitter shuts down others. Nevertheless, Twitter tries to keep terrorist groups off balance; in March 2016 alone, Twitter shut down 26,000 suspected IS-related accounts.[24]

IS is resilient, and cyberspace is so vast that it cannot be comprehensively policed. During 2015, IS was frequently relying on Telegram, a Germany-based app with a high level of encryption. Telegram sometimes blocks channels when it finds that IS is using them, but as has been the case with Twitter, IS finds new ways to reach its audiences. IS even provides tutorials to its followers so they can use chat apps that have the best encryption.[25]

When he was preparing the explosives that were used in the Brussels attacks of March 2016, Najim Laachroui communicated online with an IS commander in Syria, asking that chemicals be tested to determine the most effective composition of the bombs he would make. He also stated that several fugitives from the Paris attacks of

[23] "Unfriended," *Economist*, December 12, 2015, 47–8; Rukmini Callimachi, "A News Agency with Scoops Directly from ISIS, and a Veneer of Objectivity," *New York Times*, January 14, 2016.

[24] Christopher S. Stewart and Mark Maremont, "Twitter and Islamic State Deadlock on Social Media Battlefield," *Wall Street Journal*, April 13, 2016.

[25] Newley Purnell and Resty Woro Yuniar, "Islamic State Eludes Southeast Asian Authorities with Telegram App," *Wall Street Journal*, January 19, 2016.

the previous year had split up and were hiding in safe houses. This kind of information might have allowed security forces to pounce on the terrorists, but the communications were not detected because they were encrypted on Telegram.[26]

IS, Al Qaeda, and other terrorist organizations also have their own technicians working on encryption software. In 2013, Global Islamic Media Front (GIMF), a clearinghouse of sorts for jihadist propaganda and technology, developed first an encryption product for texting – Asrar al-Dardashah (Secrets of the Chat) – and then its Mobile Encryption Program for messages and files on mobile phones that run Android and Symbian operating systems. GIMF claimed that its software would be "a blessing, relief, and secure weapon for our brothers for continuous communication far from the eyes and monitoring of the enemies."[27] At some point, presumably, security agencies learn how to hack into these systems and then either disrupt them or allow them to continue to glean information from them.

Publicly available software also is used by extremist groups. Yopmail, which has been referred to as "the burner phone of email," gives users an e-mail address that can be used for eight days without registering it.[28] Tools such as this, which can be relied on briefly and then abandoned, have considerable appeal to IS and its kin. Sometimes a cell phone is used for only a single call and then discarded.

Old-style communication techniques sometimes come into play. Recognizing that encrypted messages may attract attention from intelligence agencies, Al Qaeda and others have at times relied

[26] Sebastian Rotella, "ISIS via WhatsApp: 'Blow Yourself Up, O Lion,'" *Frontline*, July 11, 2016, www.pbs.org/wgbh/frontline/article/isis-via-whatsapp-blow-yourself-up-o-lion/ [accessed July 25, 2016].

[27] Gil Aegerter, "Terrorists, Jihadists Get New Mobile Phone Encryption Software," *NBC News*, September 4, 2013, www.nbcnews.com/news/other/terrorists-jihadists-get-new-mobile-phone-encryption-software-f1C11073763 [accessed August 29, 2014].

[28] Patrick Tucker, "A Quick Guide to the Jihadist Communications Toolkit," *Defense One*, July 22, 2016, www.defenseone.com/technology/2016/07/quick-guide-jihadist-communications-toolkit/130159/ [accessed July 23, 2016].

on handwritten messages delivered by trusted couriers.[29] (Even this method is not wholly safe. Osama bin Laden was located partly through tracking such a courier. This was followed by the raid in which he was killed.)

As the struggle over controlling online tools continues, IS further refines its material and its dissemination. Its execution images are best known and even though they constitute only a relatively small percentage of IS online content, they illustrate sophisticated media manipulation skills. As Judith Tinnes has written, "Many mass media outlets – most notably tabloids – show unashamed voyeuristic fascination with execution footage, often ignoring the full (much broader and complex) spectrum of ideological messaging." The mass media, wrote Tinnes, serve IS "as free-of-charge multipliers for their propaganda." She added that during 2015 alone, IS executed more than 1,000 captives in front of still or video cameras.[30]

Execution footage is attention getting and generates fear, but as a recruiting tool it is likely to attract those more interested in committing murder than in building the caliphate. More common in IS online content are images showing male bonding – fighters embracing one another or otherwise exuding triumphal spirit. Shahira Fahmy wrote that "the strongest and most successful [IS] narrative is one which relates to utopianism, and imagery of brotherhood, serenity, and camaraderie." Fahmy also observed the gender imbalance in images in the IS online magazine, *Dabiq:* less than 1 percent of the photos in the magazine show women.[31]

IS media producers pattern some of their content on popular media, with IS video scenes mimicking those seen in films such as *American Sniper* and video games such as *Call of Duty.* They also

---

[29] Sam Schechner and Benoit Faucon, "New Tricks Make ISIS, Once Easily Tracked, a Sophisticated Opponent," *Wall Street Journal,* September 11, 2016.

[30] Judith Tinnes, "Counting Lives Lost – Monitoring Camera-Recorded Extrajudicial Executions by the 'Islamic State,'" *Perspectives on Terrorism* 10 (1), February 2016, 78–9.

[31] Shahira Fahmy, "Visual Cultures of Terror: Examining the Visual Communication of Islamic State," panel presentation, International Communication Association annual conference, Fukuoka, Japan, June 2016.

understand market segmentation. Javier Lesaca found that IS video producers create three different versions of their products for global audiences and twenty-six more with content that is targeted specifically at audiences from Afghanistan to West Africa. In addition to Arabic, IS material is available in English, Russian, French, and German.[32]

No other terrorist organizations – and not many governments – have matched the volume and sophistication of IS media content. This kind of productivity does not ensure ultimate victory (however IS might define that), but it does guarantee a prominent place in the global public's consciousness and establishes a precedent for other terrorist groups, present and future.

Recruiting

One of the most important uses by IS of its online capabilities is recruiting new fighters and others willing to live in the caliphate. As military pressure against IS has escalated, inflicting significant casualties and leading to desertions, IS has needed to constantly replenish its ranks. Its expansion into new territory also required additional fighters and support personnel. This process also requires a second level of recruitment: building a global base that will proselytize, raise funds, and generally promote IS while also counteracting criticism from detractors.

IS has proved itself clever and assiduous in its online recruiting. There is no shortage of prospects. Google reported in early 2016 that more than 50,000 people search for the phrase "join ISIS" every month, and Jordanian officials said that about 100 Jordanians Googled the phrase each week.[33] Presumably, many of these Googlers

---

[32] Javier Lesaca, "On Social Media, ISIS Uses Modern Cultural Images to Spread Anti-modern Values," *Brookings TechTank*, September 24, 2015, www.brookings .edu/blogs/techtank/posts/2015/09/24-isis-social-media-engagement [accessed September 26, 2015].

[33] Sheera Frenkel, "Everything You Ever Wanted to Know about How ISIS Uses the Internet," *BuzzFeed*, May 12, 2016, www.buzzfeed.com/sheerafrenkel/everything-you-ever-wanted-to-know-about-how-isis-uses-the-i?utm_term=.sh1M7zM8Q# .ba61Mp18X [accessed May 14, 2016].

are just vaguely curious about IS, but some are serious about signing up. These men and women might eventually be directed to an online handbook, "Hijrah [Emigrate] to the Islamic State: What to Pack, Who to Contact, Where to Go." Videos of foreign fighters are used to present encouraging role models to prospective recruits.

Some prospects are easily sold on the idea of joining IS. These include those who have relatives who are already in the caliphate or who are driven by their own perceptions of Islamic duty. Others may be so unhappy with their lives for political, religious, or economic reasons that they see IS as a haven where they can resurrect their lives.

Perhaps most fascinating are the cases of IS courtship of those who at the outset are more curious than enthusiastic, and whose online connection to IS begins by asking a few innocent questions. Once IS recruiters begin their relationship with the prospect through social media, they spin a cocoon of enticement and reassurance around the person and gradually offer incentives to travel to the caliphate.

In June 2015, Rukmini Callimachi of the *New York Times* wrote a detailed profile of a twenty-three-year-old American woman who was one of these prospects. During six months of online conversations, IS members spent thousands of hours with "Alex" (who adopted the pseudonym when agreeing to be interviewed by the *Times*) and sent her the Qur'an, hijabs, and even chocolate. Alex was curious about Islam, and her new online "friends" answered her questions and encouraged her interest to the point at which she converted. Alex, who led a relatively isolated existence, reveled in the new online community of which she had become a part. Eventually, her principal "friend" offered to buy Alex a ticket to Austria, where he would introduce her to her future husband, presumably an IS member who would take her to Syria. At this point, Alex's grandparents, with whom she lived, discovered what was going on and intervened. Alex did not travel to the caliphate.[34]

---

[34] Rukmini Callimachi, "ISIS and the Lonely Young American," *New York Times*, June 27, 2015.

Alex's story is far from unique, even in the United States. A George Washington University report, *ISIS in America: From Retweets to Raqqa*, which was released in December 2015, provides details of cases, most of which involve Muslim Americans (including many converts). The outcomes of these cases ranged from arrest by US authorities to death as a suicide bomber in Iraq.[35]

One of the Americans, seventeen-year-old Ali Amin, son of Yemeni immigrants, corresponded online with IS recruiters and began his own Twitter account that soon had 4,000 followers to whom he sent more than 7,000 tweets asking for financial support for IS. After he was arrested, he told the judge in charge of his case: "For the first time, I felt I was not only being taken seriously about very important and weighty topics, but was actually being asked for guidance. By assimilating into the internet world instead of the real world, I became absorbed in a 'virtual' struggle while disconnecting from what was real: my family, my life, and my future." He pleaded guilty to providing material support to a terrorist organization and was sentenced to a prison term of 136 months.[36]

In the cases of Alex, Ali, and others, the insularity of the IS cocoon created an echo chamber in which only IS litanies could be heard. These comprise stories of Muslim victimization and heroic retribution. To an outsider, their logic may seem porous, but outsiders do not enter this virtual world. Those who speak for IS are trained in the psychology of recruitment and their arguments are carefully calibrated. They retweet what they consider to be the most effective material and promote new pro-IS Twitter accounts, which is particularly important in bringing audience to new accounts that are being

[35] Lorenzo Vidino and Seamus Hughes, *ISIS in America: From Retweets to Raqqa*, George Washington University, December 2015, https://cchs.gwu.edu/sites/cchs.gwu.edu/files/downloads/ISIS%20in%20America%20-%20Full%20Report_0.pdf [accessed January 12, 2016].

[36] Scott Shane, Matt Apuzzo, and Eric Schmitt, "Americans Attracted to ISIS Find an 'Echo Chamber' on Social Media," *New York Times*, December 8, 2015; Paula Reid, "Virginia Teen Gets More Than 11 Years for Supporting ISIS," CBS News, August 28, 2015, www.cbsnews.com/news/virginia-teen-ali-amin-gets-11-years-for-supporting-isis/ [accessed August 30, 2015].

launched by previously suspended users.[37] Never before has a terrorist organization operated this kind of enterprise on such a scale.

As described in Chapter 3, IS's economy is sustained through numerous financial mechanisms including taxation and selling looted antiquities. Social media have also been essential in fundraising, with efforts including the micro "bake sale" approach of individual solicitors (such as Ali Amin) to more sophisticated ventures.

Although the major social media platforms have policies prohibiting terrorist advocacy and recruiting, most leave large loopholes that terrorist fundraisers take advantage of. Here are excerpts from some Internet companies' terms of service:

- Twitter: "You may not make threats of violence or promote violence, including threatening or promoting terrorism."
- Facebook: "There is no place on Facebook for terrorists, terrorist propaganda, or the praising of terror."
- Instagram: "Instagram is not a place to support or praise terrorism...."
- YouTube: "We have clear policies prohibiting terrorist recruitment and content intending to incite violence, and quickly remove videos violating these policies when flagged by our users."

These and other social media providers have filtering tools that can detect some violations of their policies, but fundraising appeals that are somewhat oblique are unlikely to trigger those filters. Further, social media companies do not always consult the sanctions and terrorist lists compiled by the United States and other governments.[38]

The Camstoll Group, a consulting firm specializing in sanctions and illicit finance and staffed by former US Treasury Department officials, has studied online fundraising that benefits Al Qaeda and IS. The firm found that social media offer supporters of "financial jihad" a relatively safe place to do business. By not recruiting fighters or explicitly advocating terrorist activities, these fundraisers can

[37] Vidinio and Hughes, *ISIS in America*, 24.
[38] Camstoll Group, *Use of Social Media by Terrorist Fundraisers and Financiers*, April 2016, 3, 11–12. www.camstoll.com/wp-content/uploads/2016/04/Social-Media-Report-4.22.16.pdf [accessed May 8, 2016].

operate freely, and even when their accounts are shut down by service providers, they can be up and working again with new accounts within hours. The organizer of the Popular Commission in Support of the Syrian Revolution, which raised large sums for IS and Al Nusra, had his Twitter account closed but still operated an Instagram account with more than a million followers. Other terrorist fundraisers have issued video appeals that were posted on YouTube and then disseminated through Twitter and Facebook.[39]

Kuwaiti preacher Hajjaj al-Ajmi used a Twitter campaign to urge his 250,000 followers to send money to special bank accounts set up to help IS, for "jihad, not aid." Others held auctions on Twitter to sell cars, boats, and vacation homes to fund IS. IS even offered "naming opportunities" – if you gave enough money, a IS brigade might be named in your honor.[40] IS understands crowdfunding technique, relying on videos of people speaking the language of their target audience. IS also offers advice on credit card fraud, PayPal and eBay scams, and other such tactics.[41]

The strengths of social media are also their vulnerabilities. Anyone can create a Twitter or Facebook account, and with a bit of artifice – "Help the Syrian Refugees" – that account can raise money from unsuspecting donors and from others who may know or suspect the real destination of the funds. One fundraiser whose Twitter account says it belongs to a "humanitarian and welfare organization based in Pakistan since 1997, helping alleviate the suffering of the less fortunate of its society" directs money to Al Qaeda, the Taliban, and Lashkar-e-Taibah.[42] Unless a government or other regulator has proof of this and presents it to a social media provider that will take action, this kind of operation can continue indefinitely.

---

[39] Ibid., 6–7, 10.

[40] Joby Warrick, *Black Flags: The Rise of ISIS* (New York: Doubleday, 2015), 269.

[41] *Daesh Recruitment: How the Group Attracts Supporters*, NATO Strategic Communications Centre of Excellence, November 2016, 14, www.stratcomcoe .org/daesh-recruitment-how-group-attracts-supporters-0 [accessed January 10, 2017].

[42] Camstoll Group, *Use of Social Media*, 9.

MESSAGE VERSUS MESSAGE

IS's success in using social media is dangerous on two levels. First, it has significantly enhanced IS's ability to make its case to sympathetic publics and to recruit fighters. Second, its unprecedented scope and sophistication may serve as a model for other terrorist organizations' media operations.

Recognizing this, governments have scrambled to respond, but while IS has proved itself agile and innovative, governments have been ... government-like. Plagued by bureaucratic turf battles and an inability to break free from decades-old media strategies, only by mid-2016 were some governments beginning to show signs of essential adaptability. Further complicating this were the politics of government funding. Claiming that a program was even partly a counterterrorism initiative would usually be sufficient to unlock the gates to the government treasury. With many millions in funding available for such programs, government agencies became even more parochial than usual and were loath, at least initially, to allow substantial amounts of money to flow to outsiders who might have understood the issues involved better than the people in government.

While governments of the anti-IS coalition struggled to define their tasks and craft their messaging, IS relied on more than fifty media offices in countries where it is active, with tasks assigned by the caliphate's leadership. According to Charlie Winter and Jordan Bach-Lombardo, this network "seemingly never goes off message, always transmitting the same carefully constructed ideas of the triumphant, defiant caliphate and the promise of community." Winter and Bach-Lombardo added that rather than disseminating their material only by themselves, the IS media specialists rely heavily on "unofficial spokespeople who share their media outside the caliphate's formal communications structure, encouraging others around the world to autonomously spread the Islamic State message alongside them. Because those unofficial propagandists are best-suited to identifying the ideal channel for reaching their respective local audiences – and tailoring the core narrative accordingly – the influence of the Islamic State's communications skyrockets."[43]

To bolster their case, IS media planners seek out Muslim scholars whose views and endorsement might add credibility to IS recruiting efforts. IS representatives may try to nudge those scholars closer to IS doctrine. A NATO study of this process noted that "influencing the views of one scholar ... could change the views of thousands of Muslims." The same study found the IS recruiters rely heavily on religious narratives and quotations (regardless of their original context) to support a strategy that "stresses that the defeat of the 'Islamic State' would not be due to the strength of the enemy, but rather to the weakness of the people who are still hesitating to support them." These recruiters warn against their enemies' efforts "to remove the Qur'an from Muslims' hearts." And to strengthen their message and make certain that it, and not contrary communication from others, reaches their target audience, IS urged its followers to destroy satellite dishes and portrayed outside news organizations as peddlers of intentionally false depictions of IS activities.[44]

To counteract IS communications over the longer term, lessons from counterinsurgency (COIN) may be applicable. COIN was a key part of General David Petraeus's strategy at the height of US combat operations in Iraq. David Fidler has suggested that the COIN approach of "clear, hold, and build" can be used in cyberspace. "Clear" involves shutting down IS social media content through a persistent campaign. As noted earlier, this is difficult because IS supporters quickly open new accounts when older ones are closed. But if the effort is made and incremental progress takes place, the IS voice, while not silenced, will not be so loud. "Hold" requires bringing anti-IS voices onto social media in a broader and better organized way.

[43] Charlie Winter and Jordan Bach-Lombardo, "A Unifying Theory – and Plan – for Defeating ISIS Propaganda," *Defense One*, February 15, 2016, www.defenseone .com/ideas/2016/02/unifying-theoryand-plan-defeating-isis-propaganda/125940/ [accessed February 16, 2016].
[44] *Daesh Recruitment*, 18, 20, 23–5.

"Build" necessitates developing constructive online conversations about repairing societal damage done by IS and addressing social issues that IS has used to its advantage.[45]

Such efforts are complicated by the nature of the communities involved, both pro- and anti-IS. A 2016 RAND study of Twitter content found that in the Arab world Shia Muslims condemned IS, members of the Syrian anti-Assad movement had mixed reactions to IS, and the Sunni majority (particularly in Egypt, Saudi Arabia, and other Gulf Cooperation Council states) was "highly fractured along national lines." Meanwhile, the IS messaging followed a pattern of insulting Shia, the Syrian regime, and the international community.[46]

The RAND report made several particularly important recommendations: First, that the anti-IS coalition should highlight IS atrocities because these, such as the burning alive of a Jordanian pilot in 2015, stimulated considerable anti-IS Twitter content; and second, that selecting IS opponents to train in social media techniques should be done carefully because those opponents may include members of Al Qaeda and other terrorist groups.[47]

Such suggestions about overall strategy are useful only to the extent that they serve as foundation stones on which carefully designed and tightly focused tactics are built. Among the most assertive governments in this realm are those of the United Kingdom and the United States.

United Kingdom

In September 2015, British Prime Minister David Cameron announced that the United Kingdom would wage a "propaganda war" against

---

[45] David Fidler, "Countering ISIS Extremism in Cyberspace: Time for Clear, Hold, and Build?," *Net Politics*, Council on Foreign Relations, March 12, 2015, http://blogs.cfr.org/cyber/2015/03/12/countering-isis-extremism-in-cyberspace-time-for-clear-hold-and-build/ [accessed March 20, 2015].

[46] Elizabeth Bodine-Baron, Todd C. Helmus, Madeline Magnuson, and Zev Winkelman, *Examining ISIS Support and Opposition Networks on Twitter* (Santa Monica, CA: RAND Corporation, 2016), www.rand.org/pubs/research_reports/RR1328.html [accessed January 3, 2017]. Also available in print form.

[47] Ibid.

IS. This campaign relies on "strategic communication," defined by the UK government as "the systematic and coordinated use of all means of communication to deliver UK national security objectives by influencing the attitudes and behaviors of individuals, groups, and states." Recognizing the need to prevent homegrown terrorist activity, the UK Home Office said its effort was running at "industrial pace and scale," with the goal of bringing about "attitudinal and behavioral change" among young British Muslims.[48]

As governments are wont to do, UK officialdom went overboard in this effort. The Home Office's Research, Information, and Communications Unit (RICU) led a covert program, which, according to an investigative series published by the *Guardian*, hired "linguists, psychologists, and anthropologists as well as counterterrorism strategists, digital media experts, filmmakers, and marketing consultants." Duties were divided among three units: "a monitoring and coordination team to watch and study digital and traditional media; an insight and analysis team to research audience reactions; and a domestic and international campaigns team to deliver the covert propaganda."[49] This Home Office project was in line with a Ministry of Defense doctrine describing information as "so prevalent, potent, and unavoidable that it forms as much a part of the strategic environment as the terrain or weather."[50]

The extent of the British government's involvement in some of its counterterrorism projects was masked by hiring contractors to generate and disseminate the information products under invisible government supervision. This presumably enhances credibility, but it also risks quick loss of that credibility if government direction is discovered by the projects' target audiences.

[48] Ian Cobain, Alice Ross, Rob Evans, and Mona Mahmood, "Revealed: UK's Covert Propaganda Bid to Stop Muslims Joining ISIS," *Guardian*, May 2, 2016.

[49] Ian Cobain, Alice Ross, Rob Evans, and Mona Mahmood, "Inside RICU, the Shadowy Propaganda Unit Inspired by the Cold War," *Guardian*, May 2, 2016.

[50] Ian Cobain, Alice Ross, Rob Evans, and Mona Mahmood, "How Britain Funds the 'Propaganda War' Against ISIS in Syria," *Guardian*, May 3, 2016.

One of the government ventures was a documentary film about Muslim athletes participating in the 2012 Olympic Games, which took place in London. The film was shown on fifteen television channels and was watched by an estimated 30 million Muslims worldwide. The journalists who made the film said they were not aware that the ultimate source of their funding was the British government.[51]

Another government program was creation of Help for Syria, a humanitarian project that provided aid to Syrians displaced by the war in their homeland. Among the program's principal recruits were university students in the United Kingdom, particularly British Muslims. By delivering ads to more than a million Facebook users and sending leaflets to 760,000 homes, Help for Syria wanted to encourage young people to become involved with UK-based charities rather than traveling to Syria, where they might be ensnared by IS. Although the government connection was not revealed until it was discovered by the news media, Help for Syria was designed and promoted by a RICU contractor.[52]

More transparent was the UK government's Prevent program, which organized intervention with young people who might be susceptible to radicalization. But Prevent had problems. As the BBC reported, although "security officials wanted schemes to prevent young people from following Al Qaeda's world view, other officials saw it as a means of funding pet projects ... Many groups that received funding knew what they were doing – focusing on theology and countering the politics of extremism. But others had no idea about radicalization at all." Further, according to the BBC, some Muslim clerics and community leaders felt that their neighborhoods were being unfairly targeted, a suspicion that was reinforced when it was found that Prevent money had been used to fund CCTV

[51] Ian Cobain, Alice Ross, Rob Evans, and Mona Mahood, "Government Hid Fact It Paid for 2012 Olympics Film Aimed at Muslims," *Guardian*, May 3, 2016.

[52] Ian Cobain, Alice Ross, Rob Evans, and Mona Mahmood, "Refugee Aid Drive Secretly Funded as Counter-radicalization Scheme," *Guardian*, May 4, 2016.

(closed circuit television) surveillance cameras in Muslim areas of Birmingham.[53]

The Muslim Council of Britain, representing 500 mosques, schools, and charities, responded to the government's clumsy targeting and perceived anti-Islam bias by announcing its own program, which would emphasize the case against violence. The prominence of Britain's Muslim leadership in this effort was applauded by former Metropolitan Police chief superintendent Dal Babu, himself a Muslim, who said: "It's not rocket science. Go back to how we defeated the IRA ... We needed the confidence of Catholic communities."[54]

If the struggle against terrorism is truly to be the "long war," then a multifaceted, long-term commitment is essential, and it should not be weakened at the outset by too much bureaucracy and too little oversight. The alternative to a long-term approach is to temporarily expand existing government offices' responsibilities, with the implied message that eventually the terrorist threat will pass, the political situation will return to "normal," and these offices will revert to their traditional roles.

That latter choice would reflect wishful thinking, without much grounding in reality. Governments would be well advised to establish permanent counterterrorism and related prevention programs and develop carefully designed ground rules related to transparency and privacy. If and when the terrorist threat subsides, these programs could be reduced in size or done away with. But for now, it is dangerous to view the threat of terrorism as a short-term aberration that can be "fixed" if enough money and firepower are thrown at it.

United States

In March 2016, President Obama issued an executive order creating the Global Engagement Center (GEC) within the State Department.

---

[53] Dominic Casciani, "The Prevent Strategy and Its Problems," *BBC News*, August 26, 2016, www.bbc.com/news/uk-28939555 [accessed August 30, 2016].

[54] Vikram Dodd, "Muslim Council of Britain to Set Up Alternative Counterterror Scheme," *Guardian*, October 19, 2016.

The center's responsibilities include "coordinating, integrating, and synchronizing all public communications of the United States Government directed toward foreign audiences abroad in order to counter the messaging and diminish the influence of international terrorist organizations and other violent extremists abroad." The GEC was also directed to counter "communications-related radicalization ... and recruitment activities" and to build "the capacity of partners."[55]

The State Department expanded on the executive order by noting that the center would be led by former Navy SEAL and assistant secretary of defense Michael Lumpkin. In its operations, the center would rely on third-party content as well as that generated by the US government and would provide "seed funding and other support to NGOs (nongovernmental organizations) and media startups focused on countering violent extremism messaging." Further, the GEC would be an information clearinghouse for other US agencies with similar missions.[56]

All that sounds good, but some bureaucratic context helps to understand why the GEC might be an important step forward ... and why it might not.

Ever since the 2001 attacks, the United States has moved uncertainly in its messaging directed to primarily Muslim audiences. The first effort was a series of videos about the lives of successful Muslim Americans, which was widely derided as the "Happy Muslims" campaign, and which television channels in some Muslim countries refused to air. After that, US efforts only slowly became more sophisticated, and once IS arrived on the scene the effectiveness gap between terrorist propaganda and American countermessaging grew wider. Part of the problem was that the State Department was required by law to provide a disclaimer on its online products, and credibility was

---

[55] www.federalregister.gov/articles/2016/03/17/2016–06250/developing-an-integrated-global-engagement-center-to-support-government-wide-counterterrorism [accessed March 30, 2016].

[56] US Department of State, "A New Center for Global Engagement," fact sheet, January 8, 2016, www.state.gov/r/pa/prs/ps/2016/01/251066.htm# [accessed January 15, 2016].

not enhanced by placing the State Department seal at the end of video content. One of these products was the "Think Again, Turn Away" program, which began in 2011 and focused on Twitter and YouTube. Its messages were imbued with sarcasm about the IS's treatment of fellow Muslims and its penchant for murdering innocents.

There was little evidence of this approach being effective in terms of dissuading potential IS recruits, and it may even have been counterproductive because it opened yet another online venue on which supporters of terrorist groups could comment on the US messaging. Relying on "snark" might turn out to burnish rather than undercut the IS emphasis on what it portrayed as heroic violence. Lumpkin said that such messaging was "like wrestling with a pig. The pig likes it, and you get dirty."[57]

Throughout its efforts, the State Department was careful about playing by the rules, treating its messaging as a facet of public diplomacy. But diplomatic practice is unsuited for the street fight that is the reality of dealing with terrorists. Presumably, US intelligence agencies have been quietly operating in this space as well and not leaving US government fingerprints on whatever they're doing. This leads into an issue that will be discussed later in this chapter: How much transparency is appropriate in such ventures?

Aside from any hidden work being done by the intelligence community, the main adjustment US officials made in 2016 was to provide *invisible* financial support and technical expertise to local providers of online content and let them distribute this content. Lisa Monaco, assistant to President Obama for homeland security and counterterrorism, said in early 2016 of this approach that "we know that the U.S. government is often not the best or most compelling voice" for the counterradicalization message.[58]

[57] Helene Cooper, "U.S. Drops Snark in Favor of Emotion to Undercut Extremists," *New York Times*, July 28, 2016.

[58] Lisa O. Monaco, "Evolving to Meet the New Terrorist Threat," speech at the Council on Foreign Relations, March 7, 2016, www.whitehouse.gov/the-press-office/2016/03/07/remarks-lisa-o-monaco-council-foreign-relations-kenneth-moskow-memorial [accessed March 20, 2016].

GEC director Lumpkin said that his office promptly began "hiring out content to be developed," and that the contractors, mostly NGOs, "put their own logos on it and call it their own." He added, "[T]hen we can help amplify it and hand it to other people to repurpose it, but they're kind of on their own once they've got it." As for delivery, Lumpkin planned to get help from companies that analyze big data related to Internet users and, based on that, direct the messaging to individuals who might be likely recruiting targets for extremists. This plan is similar to those used by the likes of Google and Amazon based on online browsing data.[59]

Lumpkin's team also directed a shift in emphasis in the messages' content. On Facebook, Instagram, and other social media venues, the sarcasm was dropped, replaced by emotion-driven storytelling about the impact on families of the young people who joined IS and never returned home.

Beyond government outreach, some independent ventures have contributed to antiradicalization discourse. A joint project between the University of California, San Diego, and the Independent University, Bangladesh, worked with young Bangladeshi filmmakers on cinema projects with creative anti-extremist messages. Robert Hooper, who directed the program, wrote: "Effective counterterrorism must come from *within* the communities facing extremism. The young artists, writers, bloggers, and filmmakers who live and work among potential terrorists must drive the efforts to counter violent ideology. Capacity building in local institutions and among individuals capable of leading the fight against violent extremism will succeed in gaining traction where other measures have failed. The Islamic State is fighting and winning a war of images and ideas by using 21st century technologies to promote medieval messages. Arming talented young students with the same persuasive weapons – cameras,

---

[59] Kimberly Dozier, "Anti-ISIS-Propaganda Czar's Ninja War Plan: We Were Never Here," *Daily Beast*, March 15, 2016, www.thedailybeast.com/articles/2016/03/15/obama-s-new-anti-isis-czar-wants-to-use-algorithms-to-target-jihadis.html [accessed March 18, 2016].

lights, microphones, laptops, and counter narratives – can help these communities win the war against violent extremism."[60]

Given the growth of terrorist organizations' capabilities during the past decade, the US government's new emphasis on innovation and flexibility, although belated, along with Britain's commitment to covert projects, point to the path that counterterrorist measures will likely follow during the coming years. Realism is displacing wishful thinking.

As these efforts develop further, the distinction between "counterterrorism," measures taken against active terrorist organizations or individuals, and "countering violent extremism," measures to prevent enlistment in terrorist groups, is increasingly artificial. A holistic approach toward terrorism makes better sense, and "counterterrorism" can be all-encompassing. The terrorists' active involvement continuum starts with the wooing of sympathetic individuals through online and other media and extends to some of those individuals wielding rifles or wearing suicide vests. Intervention as early as possible is the best course, but even the IS fighter on the battlefield might be induced to desert, and so the countermessaging must be persistent and directed to those at all levels of terrorist involvement.

DISRUPTING TERRORIST MEDIA

Extremists' presence on online media must be monitored and disrupted, but it should be kept in mind that intelligence agencies may prefer that at least some online sites and conversations not be shut down entirely. They provide useful insights about extremist mentality and tactics, and they also may leave footprints that can be followed to find even more information.

For the most part, however, effective counterterrorism measures require destroying, or at least severely hampering, terrorists' abilities to communicate with one another and with the broader

---

[60] Robert Hooper, "How Film School Can Address Violent Extremism," *Georgetown Journal of International Affairs*, January 29, 2016, http://journal.georgetown.edu/how-film-school-can-address-violent-extremism/ [accessed March 30, 2016].

public, especially potential recruits. As noted in the preceding text, IS has proved exceptionally proficient at using various forms of media. Countering this messaging has been only partially successful, due mainly to the scope of IS activity. The US government in 2016 pointed proudly to Twitter having shut down 125,000 accounts that were determined to be IS-related, but consider what that really means: 125,000 is a staggering number, and IS certainly had far more than those that were identified and closed. Further, opening a new Twitter account to replace one that was closed can be done in a matter of minutes, and followers will presumably find it.

To truly get ahead of IS and other terrorist organizations, governments must use the superior technologies they can access and sustain a "cyber war" against terrorists. US Secretary of Defense Ashton Carter said in February 2016, "Our use of cyber ... particularly in Syria [is] to interrupt, disrupt, ISIL's command and control, to cause them to lose confidence in their networks, to overload their networks so they can't function, and do all of these things that will interrupt their ability to command and control forces there, to control the population and the economy."[61]

This approach has multiple goals. One is to discourage IS leaders from relying on online internal communication, particularly encrypted messaging, and push them back to using cell phones, calls from which can be monitored and tracked, and other methods susceptible to detection.

Making terrorists doubt their online security is useful, and even more valuable may be hacking into their computers through "spear phishing," which is sending e-mails from what appear to be trusted sources but that have infected attachments, and "watering hole" attacks that put malicious software on websites the terrorists visit. Once the infection takes hold, this software can give US government hackers

[61] Sydney J. Freedberg Jr., "Cyber War Against ISIL Hones Weapons vs. Russia, China," *Breaking Defense*, February 29, 2016, http://breakingdefense.com/2016/02/cyber-war-against-isil-is-model-for-other-threats/ [accessed March 2, 2016].

access to the computers' contents.[62] When inside the computers, the hackers can learn about IS commanders' online habits and even alter their messages, sending IS fighters to places where they would be vulnerable to attacks by drones or other weapons.[63]

Cyber war is still in its infancy, and as such its value should not be overrated by referring to "dropping cyber bombs" and other such terminology that seems to equate cyber tactics with kinetic combat. Some cyber war tactics can cause actual physical damage, as with "Stuxnet," a computer worm, believed to have been created by joint American–Israeli research, which was discovered in 2010 to have infected several Iranian industrial facilities, including a uranium enrichment site. Centrifuges used to enrich uranium gas were failing frequently due to Stuxnet's effects on the computers controlling those centrifuges. This temporarily slowed Iran's nuclear program.[64]

Overall, cyber warfare's true value – as of now – is to degrade and disrupt an enemy's functions that rely on information and communication technologies (ICTs).[65] Given that IS counts heavily on ICTs for everything from its financial operations to its command and control in combat, cyber war might have considerable impact.

Looking ahead, defense ministry strategists around the world know that cyber warfare will be relied on more heavily in future conflicts, not only against the likes of IS but also in confrontations between major powers. The United States, China, and Russia are among the countries expanding their cyber war capacities, and the next step may be to define when cyber mischief becomes cyber *war* in

---

[62] Shane Harris and Nancy A. Youssef, "U.S. Ratchets Up Cyber Attacks on ISIS," *Daily Beast*, April 17, 2016, www.thedailybeast.com/articles/2016/04/17/u-s-ratchets-up-cyber-attacks-on-isis.html [accessed April 19, 2016].

[63] David E. Sanger, "U.S. Unleashes Digital Arsenal in War with ISIS," *New York Times*, April 25, 2016.

[64] Kim Zetter, "An Unprecedented Look at Stuxnet, the World's First Digital Weapon," *Wired*, November 3, 2014, www.wired.com/2014/11/countdown-to-zero-day-stuxnet/ [accessed November 10, 2014].

[65] Brandon Valeriano, Heather Roff, and Sean Lawson, "Stop Saying We're Dropping 'Cyber Bombs' on ISIS," *Defense One*, May 24, 2016, www.defenseone.com/ideas/2016/05/stop-saying-were-dropping-cyber-bombs-isis/128581/ [accessed May 25, 2016].

the sense of requiring a comparable response. When Russia interfered with the 2016 US presidential election, the American government imposed sanctions on Russia. What happens when cyber meddling is ratcheted up to the point of significantly damaging a country's electronic infrastructure? Such a conflict is unprecedented on a large scale, although some of the measures being used against IS may be precursors of future cyber combat tactics.

BOUNDARIES – PRIVACY AND ETHICS

As noted earlier in this chapter, between mid-2015 and early 2016, Twitter deleted 125,000 accounts for "threatening or promoting terrorist acts, primarily related to ISIS." The process that was followed remains something of a mystery. Twitter noted that "there is no 'magic algorithm' for identifying terrorist content on the internet, so global online platforms are forced to make challenging judgment calls based on very limited information and guidance."[66]

So, what is "terrorist content"? Suppose someone sends a tweet stating, "I think Islamic State is great." Assuming that this is an isolated statement and that there are no other tweets in this person's account related to terrorism, should Twitter shut down the account, or would that be encroaching on free speech? If, however, Twitter finds a tweet that says, "I am going to Syria to join Islamic State and I am looking for like-minded people to join me," that is definite enough about engaging in a terrorism-related act to justify Twitter not only closing the account but also notifying law enforcement authorities about the tweet.

There is a great deal of territory between those two tweets. The first one – ill-advised but probably harmless – points to the difficulty of trying to create an algorithm for policing content. As governments put more pressure on social media companies to help in combating terrorism, civil liberties advocates worry about this evolving

---

[66] "Combating Violent Extremism," *Twitter Blog*, February 5, 2016, https://blog. twitter.com/2016/combating-violent-extremism [accessed February 12, 2016].

partnership and resulting infringements on political speech. In addition to determining what speech should be prohibited and reported to the government, media companies are also considering what, if any, steps should be taken to change security features on devices such as cell phones to allow "backdoor" access by law enforcement.

In March 2016, a group of civil liberties organizations sent a letter to senior Obama administration officials asking to be allowed to participate in discussions about these matters. The letter pointed to potential ripple effects: "When the government sits down secretly with those companies that have practical control over a broad swath of public speech and private communication, and especially if and when those conversations lead to voluntary surveillance or censorship measures that would be illegal or unconstitutional for the government to undertake itself, the consequences are truly global. The U.S. government may embolden abusive governments around the world to continue exerting pressure on tech companies to assist on crackdowns on dissent and the targeting of human rights defenders."[67]

Encryption is at the center of much of this debate. After the 2015 terrorist attack in San Bernardino, California, the US government secured a court order directing Apple to help the FBI find a "backdoor" into the shooters' iPhone. Apple CEO Tim Cook objected and published an open letter that reminded the public of how much personal information can be found on cell phones and why it is important to protect that information from hackers and criminals. He wrote: "Specifically, the FBI wants us to make a new version of the iPhone operating system, circumventing several important security features ... In the wrong hands, the software – which does not exist today – would have the potential to unlock any iPhone in someone's physical possession." He added that this "would be the equivalent of a master key, capable of opening hundreds of millions of locks."[68]

---

[67] https://static.newamerica.org/attachments/12750-civil-society-letter-on-combatting-violent-extremism/WH_CVE_letter_Final_clean.9c6ef85e69fd4a9492455f65118c227f.pdf [accessed July 30, 2015].

[68] www.apple.com/customer-letter/ [accessed February 18, 2016].

The dispute promised to lead to a lengthy court battle, but in March 2016 the FBI announced that it had found a way into the terrorists' iPhone without Apple's help.

Because the communication technology at the heart of the iPhone is relatively new, many people might not realize how much of their private lives could be accessed by someone who could hack into their phones. This issue is yet another example of how terrorism affects concentric rings of societal standards. Even governments that are not fundamentally "abusive" might be tempted to extend their reach deeper into areas their citizens consider private.

In another case, in December 2015, the European Union agreed to a provisional policy to make Passenger Name Record (PNR) data available "for the prevention, detection, investigation, and prosecution of terrorist offenses and serious crime."[69] The United States has a similar policy.[70]

PNR data includes a traveler's itinerary and related information that is contained in airlines' computer reservation systems. The general public would probably pay little attention to this information being accessed and might welcome yet another antiterrorism initiative that could, among other results, make flying safer. Some people, however, might see this as an intrusion by government into private matters. Why should the government keep records about the details of your travels, including mundane matters such as your frequent flyer program numbers? This case illustrates why some civil libertarians worry about mission creep in governments' efforts to prevent terrorism by chipping away at privacy.

The media tools employed by today's terrorists are far more sophisticated and useful than those used just a few years ago, when Osama bin Laden was sending videotapes from his hideouts to television stations. Social media have transformed the reach and level

[69] www.europarl.europa.eu/news/en/news-room/20150123BKG12902/EU-Passenger-Name-Record-(PNR)-proposal-an-overview [accessed February 20, 2016].

[70] www.cbp.gov/sites/default/files/documents/pnr_privacy.pdf [accessed December 12, 2013].

of success of terrorist recruitment and have been integral in the operations of IS as a virtual state and a military force.

Media-related tactics have been integral to terrorists' success, but they also can be used to enlist public support against terrorism and help young people build better, peaceful lives. The following chapter looks toward the future and the ways that society might find a path to emerge from the era of terrorism.

5   What Lies Ahead?

The evolution of modern terrorism is illustrated in the multifaceted operations of IS. As of this writing, in early 2017, IS has suffered battlefield defeats, most notably the loss of Fallujah after a lengthy siege by Iraqi forces, and after a battle lasting many months is being pushed out of Mosul, the largest city it has held. Raqqa will be the next target, and although attacking it will be complicated by the larger war within Syria, IS will not be able to hold out indefinitely against the military heft of even limited participation by the United States, Russia, and Turkey.

Of greater concern to the countries arrayed against IS is the likelihood that battlefield defeat will trigger terror attacks elsewhere. After IS was driven out of Fallujah, a series of attacks directed or inspired by IS killed hundreds of civilians in Turkey, Saudi Arabia, Iraq, Bangladesh, and France. The level of IS's involvement in each of these attacks might vary, but certainly IS has done much to shape the global political environment in which such terroristic activity has become so frighteningly commonplace.

And while IS fights for survival on the battlefield, a rejuvenated and wiser Al Qaeda is in the wings, assembling the political pieces it needs to establish its own version of a caliphate. Although Al Qaeda has for the moment focused on this task rather than planning or commissioning new attacks in Europe or North America, it certainly has the capability to renew a far-reaching terror campaign.

IS still garners most of the headlines, but terrorism more broadly continues to grow stronger and more sophisticated.

TERRORISM GLOBALIZED

IS built its fighting force with recruits from around the world. (Al Qaeda, Al Shabaab, and some other terrorist groups have also attracted foreign fighters, but not in the numbers that have flocked to IS.) Although the highly publicized battlefield setbacks IS has suffered have undoubtedly deterred some prospective recruits and led to desertion by others, the appeal of IS should not be underrated. A December 2015 report by The Soufan Group stated that between 27,000 and 31,000 people from at least eighty-six countries had traveled to Syria and Iraq to join IS and other extremist groups. The report also pointed to Russia and Central Asia as a growing source of fighters, with numbers from there up 300 percent between mid-2014 and 2016. Further, the report noted that significant numbers of IS fighters from Western countries were returning home, with unknown agendas. Would they abandon terrorist activity or carry out new attacks?[1] IS has trained thousands of people, and if even a small percentage of these return to their homelands with instructions to wreak havoc, they could do tremendous damage.

For the foreseeable future, Syria will remain anarchic and Iraq may face renewed Sunni–Shia conflict. In such conditions, IS (or its remnants), Al Qaeda, or other extremist groups will find this region hospitable. Much less predictable is the evolution of terrorism more generally. IS, with its ability to declare a "caliphate" and then seize, hold, and govern, however bloodily, large amounts of territory has transformed the domain of terrorism from its previous manifestations of secretive groups that organize and sponsor attacks, and then run and hide. Among the possible next steps of IS or others might be acquisition of deadlier tools.

Could a terrorist group acquire nuclear material, and if so, could that material be weaponized? Security of nuclear material is a

---

[1] Soufan Group, "Foreign Fighters," December 2015, 4, http://soufangroup.com/wp-content/uploads/2015/12/TSG_ForeignFightersUpdate3.pdf [accessed January 30, 2016].

constant concern that governments usually address by saying there is nothing to worry about. But breaches of that security continue. In 2012, an eighty-two-year-old nun, Sister Megan Rice, and two fellow activists broke into the Y-12 National Security complex in Oak Ridge, Tennessee, and painted antiwar slogans on the exterior walls of the Highly Enriched Uranium Materials Facility. Security experts called this the biggest security breach in the history of the nation's atomic complex.[2] A nun and two colleagues armed with flashlights, bolt cutters, and paint brushes – not exactly a fierce team of terrorists. But although security measures at the Oak Ridge facility were upgraded after this, the ease with which entry was forced is disturbing.

More worrisome were events in Belgium, where an employee left his job at the Doel-4 nuclear power reactor to join IS in Syria, and the home of a researcher at the SCK-CEN nuclear facility was under video surveillance by two of the bombers in the 2016 Brussels airport attack. SCK-CEN holds a large supply of radioisotopes, which are used primarily by hospitals but could possibly be made parts of a "dirty bomb" that would spew radioactive material and could make an area uninhabitable for a lengthy period.[3]

Nuclear terrorism has long been the ultimate fear of counterterrorism officials (and has been the subject of numerous novels and movies). That terrorists could build their own device capable of a large nuclear explosion is unlikely, but far more feasible is their ability to buy or steal one. The Soviet Union's nuclear weapons have not all been fully accounted for, and scientists in Pakistan and elsewhere have the know-how to produce a weapon. Besides acquiring nuclear material, an attack on a nuclear reactor within the United States is a possibility.

In October 2011, just a month after Al Qaeda's attacks on the United States, the CIA informed President George W. Bush of a

---

[2] William J. Broad, "The Nun Who Broke into the Nuclear Sanctum," *New York Times*, August 10, 2012.

[3] Nancy Ing and Alexander Smith, "Brussels Attacks: Bombers Filmed Nuclear Researcher, Expert Says," *NBC News*, March 24, 2016, www.nbcnews.com/ storyline/brussels-attacks/brussels-attacks-bombers-filmed-nuclear-researcher-expert-says-n544776 [accessed March 28, 2016].

report that Al Qaeda had smuggled a ten-kiloton nuclear device into New York City. The CIA had no independent confirmation of this report, which had come from one of its agents, but the agency considered it plausible. If such a bomb were to explode around midday in the Times Square area, the casualty count could surpass one million.[4]

As it turned out, the report was a false alarm, but just as the 9/11 attacks had raised the bar in terms of mass killings by terrorists, it is reasonable to assume that terrorists will grow ever more ambitious. Given that their goal is not just to kill but also to *terrorize* and prove how formidable they are, consider the psychological impact of a nuclear explosion not only on those the terrorists considered enemies, but also on those whom they wanted to recruit. If IS – or, for that matter, any other current or future terrorist group – could use a nuclear weapon in this way, its credibility as a major world player, albeit a nefarious one, would be established and so would the presumed viability of the caliphate. The 9/11 attacks enhanced Al Qaeda's stature among its sympathizers because it had inflicted pain on the imperial giant. Spectacular attacks can give other groups a similar boost. To some extent, terrorism is public relations.

All this is speculative, and the prospect is so forbidding that our instinct is to dismiss this kind of threat as too farfetched to worry about. But realism is not fearmongering, and the issue has attracted the likes of former US senators Sam Nunn and Richard Lugar, and Harvard University's Graham Allison has proposed checklists of priorities for the White House, Congress, and the public that could intensify focus on preventing acts of nuclear terrorism.[5] As recently as April 2016, President Obama revealed that terrorists had been able to purchase isotopes from online brokers. This led to fears that a drone could spread radioactive material over heavily populated areas.[6]

---

[4] Graham Allison, *Nuclear Terrorism* (New York: Times Books, 2004), 1–4.

[5] Ibid., 205–9.

[6] Gabriel Weimann, "Terrorist Migration to the Dark Web," *Perspectives on Terrorism* 10 (3), June 2016, 43, www.terrorismanalysts.com/pt/index.php/pot/article/view/513/1013 [accessed July 8, 2016].

Perhaps even more likely than nuclear terrorism is an attack with a biological or chemical weapon, the components of which are more easily obtained and handled than is nuclear material. Toxins such as ricin might be impractical to use on a large scale, but they could be employed against small numbers of people – such as by using an aerosol spray on travelers on a subway – and would be effective as a terrorizing tool.

As one more facet of terrorism's future, cyberattacks could, at least theoretically, wreak havoc with technologies on which people depend in everyday life. Debate continues about how much damage could be done by terrorist geeks (or, for that matter, established nations) determined to damage technological infrastructure. Some say that the worst that could happen would be that ATMs wouldn't operate for a while, but others raise the specter of electrical and communications grids being crippled, creating chaos in economic and public safety sectors.

Despite the difficult-to-calculate damage that these modern weapons might inflict, it is important to remember how much destruction can be caused by "traditional" terrorist weapons – the dynamite vest or the car bomb. Ingredients for these are not difficult to acquire. Remember that the bomb that killed 168 people and did so much damage to the Oklahoma City Federal Building and nearby structures in 1995 was composed of fertilizer, diesel fuel, and a few chemicals, and the bombs at the Boston Marathon in 2013 were contained in ordinary kitchen pressure cookers. Someone determined to commit a terrorist act can find plenty of bomb-making directions and other instruction on the Internet.

While terrorists seek to expand their destructive capabilities, counterterrorism tacticians are finding new technologies helpful in their own efforts. Mapping software is being adapted to indicate areas that should be searched for weapons caches and terrorist hideouts. Geoprofiling programs crunch data about attacks and are enhanced with information about roads and terrain as well as political information. When terrorists use smartphones and other devices that have global positioning system software, analysts may find geocodes, indicating precise locations, on photographs and other material posted online.[7]

Although terrorist groups such as IS have proved themselves adept at using new technologies, they almost certainly will not be able to keep up with the research and counterterrorism product development that their enemies can muster. Universities, think tanks, high-tech companies, and other knowledge centers contribute to counterterrorism efforts. To avoid detection, terrorists may alter their patterns of operation, including their own reliance on high-tech tools, in ways that will reduce their ability to mount operations and communicate with one another.

That would be helpful, but only a step on a long path. Meanwhile, terrorism is spreading into areas where authorities have limited expertise. Governments find themselves facing the difficult task of trying to block radicalization of neophytes while dealing with experienced terrorists. Despite all the attention paid to the Middle East, particularly the IS presence in Syria and Iraq, terrorist groups have been gaining footholds elsewhere. Africa, which in many places has weak central governments and deeply flawed civil society, is especially vulnerable to terrorist incursions.

By mid-2016, Libya was the continent's northern base for terrorists associated with IS. IS organizers from the Syria–Iraq war zone set up shop in Libya, where their ranks quickly grew to include about 6,500 fighters. As IS's battlefield fortunes suffered in the center of the caliphate, prospective African recruits were told to go to Libya instead of heading for Raqqa. Given the chaotic factionalism in post-Qaddafi Libya, that seemed a good choice; in a country with countless marauding militias, terrorist groups blend in with the scenery. In ways similar to their operations in Iraq and Syria, IS officials set up a government of sorts in the Libyan territory they controlled, taxing businesses and taking part in lucrative migrant-smuggling from

---

[7] "Shrinking the Haystack," *Economist*, January 16, 2016, 86–7.

Libya to Europe. IS also began using social media recruitment aimed at African Muslims.

But Libyan groups opposing IS gradually came together. President Obama observed, "There's a whole bunch of constituencies who are hardened fighters and don't ascribe to ISIS or their perverted ideology. But they have to be organized and can't be fighting each other." The United States and other members of the anti-IS coalition provided military assistance to the Libyan faction that seemed most likely to succeed in combating IS. This was part of a larger anti-IS effort in Africa, with the United States spending US$200 million to strengthen North and West African militaries and build a drone base in Niger to allow aerial intelligence-gathering and targeting in much of that region.[8]

However Libya's future may evolve, terrorism is certain to persist in Africa, with groups ranging from IS and Al Qaeda affiliates to small independent bands. Nigeria-based Boko Haram has sent girls posing as refugees and boys as young as eight on suicide bombing missions.[9] In Senegal, which has been a source of some IS fighters in Libya, military advisors from the United States, Estonia, the Netherlands, and Austria have been training Senegalese forces in antiterrorism techniques.[10] Trying a less militarized approach, Kenya, which has been victimized by terrorist attacks mounted by Somalia-based Al Shabaab, has encouraged school programs to counter radicalization of young people, particularly among the displaced Somalis living in Kenya.[11]

In South and Southeast Asia, terrorist activity has been mostly at low levels but persistent. AQIS has tried to foment militancy among India's 180 million Muslims and exacerbate Muslim–Hindu

[8] Eric Schmitt, "U.S. Scrambling to Contain Growing ISIS Threat in Libya," *New York Times*, February 21, 2016.
[9] Dionne Searcy, "Nigeria Vexed by Boko Haram's Use of Women as Suicide Bombers," *New York Times*, February 11, 2016.
[10] Eric Schmitt, "U.S. and Dutch Train Senegal Force as Terror Fears Grow," *New York Times*, February 16, 2016.
[11] Alexis Okeowo, "Teaching Anti-Extremism in Kenya," *New Yorker*, May 26, 2016.

tensions. An IS video in Tagalog, Malay, and Bahasa Indonesia urged jihadists who could not travel to the Middle East to instead go to the Philippines, where Muslim separatists on Mindanao have battled local police and military, and where an IS affiliate might take root. Malaysian and Indonesian fighters in IS territory have urged their compatriots at home to organize attacks. Particularly worrisome to Malaysian authorities are the dozens of former members of the country's military who have volunteered to become IS fighters.[12]

In southernmost Eastern Europe, Chechnya has proved a significant source of IS fighters. Chechen law enforcement officials estimate that up to 4,000 Chechens have traveled to IS outposts in Syria and Iraq. Within Chechnya, the government of Ramzan Kadyrov has dealt as harshly with IS sympathizers, including returning fighters, as it has with Chechnya's internal insurgency.[13] Elsewhere, in Central Asia, where Islam had been banned during the early days of the Soviet Union, contemporary militancy has developed from its roots in the fight against the Soviets in Afghanistan. Today in parts of the region Muslims remain subject to various controls: bans on talking about religion outside of mosque, carrying an unauthorized Qu'ran, having a beard, wearing Islamic dress, and so forth. Not surprisingly, this has driven some Muslims underground and raised the temperature of their militancy.[14] This drew particular attention when a Uzbekistan native was charged with the 2016 New Year's Eve attack in Istanbul that killed thirty-nine persons, allegedly on behalf of IS.

Looking ahead, perhaps the most important development among terrorist organizations is the continued resilience and adaptability of Al Qaeda. IS's viciousness and skill at media manipulation has captured much of the public's attention since 2014. Its gruesome videos, the attacks it has directed or inspired, and its willingness to

---

[12] "Jihad's New Frontier," *Economist*, July 9, 2016, 34; David Ignatius, "Southeast Asia Could Be a Haven for Displaced Islamic State Fighters," *Washington Post*, August 18, 2016.

[13] Joshua Yaffa, "Chechnya's ISIS Problem," *New Yorker*, February 12, 2016.

[14] Amanda Erickson, "How the USSR's Effort to Destroy Islam Created a Generation of Radicals," *Washington Post*, January 5, 2017.

engage in conventional warfare are magnets for news coverage and counterterrorism efforts. Al Qaeda, meanwhile, in the years since conducting the most visible act of terrorism in history – the 9/11 attacks on the United States – and since the death of Osama bin Laden has committed itself to ensuring its permanence. That means not putting its supporters directly in the way of major military forces, as IS has done, and, at least for now, not provoking the United States or other enemies by attacking their homelands.

In mid-2016, Al Qaeda's leader, Ayman al-Zawahiri, criticized what he called IS's "abyss of extremism, infidel-branding, and forbidden blood," while Al Qaeda worked to unify Sunnis. Robert Ford, a former US ambassador to Syria, said Al Qaeda had matured since the days when Abu Musab al-Zarqawi was running the parent of IS, Al Qaeda in Iraq. "I am very impressed," said Ford, "by how much [they] have learned from their mistakes and their bad experiences in Iraq. They are much less brutal in Syria than they were in Iraq, and they work with non-jihadi factions, which Al Qaeda in Iraq never did ... It's going to be a much harder job to develop forces to fight them, and it's going to be a much harder job to develop public support for that."[15]

Al Qaeda has positioned itself as a leader of the effort to remove the Assad regime in Syria. While declared Assad opponents such as the United States and Turkey dither, Al Qaeda and its allies are portraying themselves as remaining resolute. Al Qaeda's latest incarnation in Syria, Jabhat Fatah al-Sham (Front for the Conquest of the Levant) has, like IS, stepped into the anarchic void to provide basic services in areas that it controls. It operates or supervises road paving, water and electricity supplies, police, food supplies, health care, rent control, and Islamic education.[16]

Not surprisingly, managing an array of jihadist groups does not always go smoothly. Al Qaeda has dual objectives – removing Assad

[15] Yaroslav Trofimov, "What Happens after ISIS Falls?," *Wall Street Journal*, September 9, 2016.
[16] "The Other Jihadist State," *Economist*, September 17, 2016, 57.

and building up its own long-term base in the region. For the former, it has built mini-coalitions, such as Ahrar al-Sham ("Free People of the Levant"), which governs areas it holds through shariah courts and is clearly committed to Al Qaeda. But the group claims that Al Qaeda does not have operational control over it, and it assisted Turkey in an anti-Assad offensive. This led to some of its units departing and associating with more doctrinaire Al Qaeda allies.[17] All very confusing, and the story has certainly been tweaked as it passed through numerous sources. But, assuming there is some truth to the tale, it illustrates how loyalties shift and how difficult it is to distinguish "bad guys" from "good guys" (if any of the latter exist).

Al Qaeda has not gone soft. It still wants to "bleed America to death" and deals ruthlessly with those who try to obstruct it. And it still aspires to building a caliphate that will be the heart of Sunni Islam. It may understand, better than IS does, that remaining a player for the long haul requires marshalling resources and not picking fights it cannot win. Patience is not a common trait among terrorist leaders, but Al Qaeda seems to value it.

IS, Al Qaeda, and other terrorist organizations share an interest in refilling their ranks after depletion by death or desertion. Among the best sources of recruits are prisons, which have proved to be fertile ground for radicalization. Some European prisons hold a disproportionate number of Muslims, and prisoner-on-prisoner radicalization is intense. In France, where about 8 percent of the national population is Muslim, 50 to 60 percent of the country's 67,000 prison inmates are Muslim. Those convicted of terrorism-related charges often become in-house bosses, dictating behavior (such as forbidding listening to music) and supervising instruction in their version of Islamic principles. Isolating known jihadists might limit their contact with the general prison population, but prison officials worry that such segregation might lead to experienced terrorists plotting

---

[17] Jennifer Cafarella, Nicholas A. Heras, and Genevieve Casagrande, "Al Qaeda Is Gaining Strength in Syria," September 1, 2016, http://foreignpolicy.com/2016/09/01/al-qaeda-is-gaining-strength-in-syria/ [accessed September 2, 2016].

together. Efforts to counter radicalization have been hampered by a shortage of Muslim prison chaplains: just 178 for the entire national prison population (while there are 684 Catholic chaplains).[18]

Much more is going on that is not visible to the public. Local as well as national law enforcement agencies around the world now devote time and resources to preventing terrorist attacks within their countries. Their efforts include "soft" measures, such as counter-radicalization efforts, and conventional intelligence gathering that may lead to arrests. But no matter how diligent law enforcement personnel may be and how many potential acts of violence they prevent, the arithmetic works against them. Someone with the worst intentions will almost inevitably slip through the counterterrorism net. Recognizing that likelihood engenders fatalism concerning the efficacy of prevention measures, but law enforcement personnel and others in related fields know that they must push on and not succumb to defeatism.

EVOLVING MEDIA USE

Those who we might call "top-level terrorists" – among them the leaders of IS and Al Qaeda and their subsidiaries – survive because they are quick to adapt to changes in the physical and virtual battlespace. For some of their online communication, this has meant moving from the easily accessible "surface web" to the "deep web" and then on to its deepest part, the "dark web." This is a part of the online universe that features drug dealing, pornography, weapons sales, and other illegal activity that its perpetrators want to hide from investigators. The dark web is out of reach of the most common search engines, such as Google, and is difficult for hackers to penetrate. IS warehouses its propaganda videos and other material on dark sites, and has raised and transferred money using the dark web's currency of choice, Bitcoin.[19]

---

[18] Noemie Bisserbe, "European Prisons Fueling Spread of Islamic Radicalism," *Wall Street Journal*, July 31, 2016; "Caged Fervour," *Economist*, September 17, 2016, 49–50.

[19] Weimann, "Terrorist Migration," 40–43.

Similarly, IS has relied on Telegram, one of the encrypted communication tools that provides enhanced security for texts and other messaging, such as instructions about how to find a particular dark web address. In 2015, Telegram began featuring "channels" for specialized content, which IS promptly started using. In March 2016 alone, 700 new IS-related channels were opened. One such channel was "Mujahideen Secrets," which provided indoctrination and information for prospective "lone wolf" terrorists.[20]

Counterterrorism experts constantly seek ways to undermine terrorists' reliance on online dissemination of information. Videos made by the US-born Yemeni imam, Anwar al-Awlaki, make the case that the United States is waging war on Islam and why it is every Muslim's duty to kill Americans.[21] Although Awlaki was killed by a US drone strike in 2011, his videos can still be accessed, although YouTube has tried to remove as many as possible. His messages are considered highly influential in encouraging attacks. To cleanse the Internet of such videos and the graphically violent imagery of IS, a new technology called "robust hashing" has been developed that analyzes individual images and assigns each a 144-digit signature. The technique's developer estimates that it can examine up to 50 million images a day. "Robust hashing" is a descendant of "PhotoDNA," which is used by companies such as Facebook and Twitter to find and remove child pornography from social media. The newer technique can be applied to video and audio files as well as photographs and can help service providers find and remove terrorists' video messaging.[22]

On a less technologically sophisticated level, social media companies are offering training to Muslim and other NGOs so they can counter extremists' online content by presenting religious and

---

[20] Michael Barak, "The Telegram Chat Software as an Arena of Activity to Encourage the 'Lone Wolf' Phenomenon," International Institute for Counter-Terrorism, May 24, 2016, www.ict.org.il/Article/1673/the-telegram-chat-software-as-an-arena-of-activity-to-encourage-the-lone-wolf-phenomenon [accessed June 18, 2016].

[21] Scott Shane, "The Lessons of Anwar al-Awlaki," *New York Times Magazine*, August 27, 2015.

[22] "Halting the Hate," *Economist*, June 25, 2016, 70–71.

social guidance to young Muslims who might be susceptible to messaging from IS and other such groups.[23] Although general anti-IS social media content has increased significantly, grassroots counter-messaging lags. To thwart terrorist recruiting and push back against young Muslims' feelings of being marginalized, positive social media discourse must become commonplace. To aid these efforts, reported *Huffington Post*, YouTube tutors video bloggers and directors "on everything from camera angles and continuity to search engine optimization, best practices for headlines, and how to go viral."[24]

As discussed in Chapter 4, extremists increasingly rely on media to recruit, fundraise, and spread their messages. White supremacist groups have reportedly studied IS and other media-savvy terrorists' online products for tips on how to make their own efforts more productive. For years, neo-Nazis and similar extremists have been expanding their media offerings, such as "hate rock" recordings, and, like IS, connecting to prospective recruits through online propaganda and conversation.

The anger that fuels extremism can be contagious, and so can extremists' methods. The jihadi in Syria and the skinhead in Britain have more in common than might seem possible. In addition to their shared tilt toward destructiveness, they both are likely to consume and disseminate social media content.

The evolution of extremism is closely linked to the evolution of media use. This process is not new. In the 1930s, the Nazis built their power through media: Hitler's use of radio, hate-filled newspapers such as *Der Sturmer*, Goebbels's pervasive propaganda – these and other tools were used to construct a society imbued with intolerance and violence. Today, the tools have become more sophisticated and even more capable of spreading poisonous lies. IS's caliphate is intrinsically fraudulent; it rides roughshod over the principles of

---

23 Tamara Audi, "Muslim Leaders, Tech Companies Work to Counter Militants," *Wall Street Journal*, March 22, 2015.

24 Jaweed Kaleem, "YouTube's Battle against ISIS," *Huffington Post*, August 24, 2015, www.huffingtonpost.com/entry/youtube-battle-against-isis_us_55d61416e4b0ab468da037a6 [accessed August 27, 2015].

Islam and wraps its thuggery in a gauze of religiosity. It has been successful in this largely because its leadership understands media use better than its opponents do.

Al Qaeda during the early bin Laden years was also adept at media manipulation, but that was before the arrival of social media. Recruiting, training, fundraising, and other functions can today be carried out online with relative ease, whether the audience is a mass constituency or an individual. Considering just the twenty-first-century jump in media use from Al Qaeda to IS, if media technology continues to evolve at a similar pace, it will further enhance terrorists' destructive capabilities and make terrorism even more difficult to defeat.

A related issue concerns new Internet vulnerabilities that terrorists might use to their advantage. One of these centers on the "Internet of things." By 2020, there are expected to be anywhere from 20 billion to 50 billion Internet-connected devices. If terrorists could hack into this system, their potential for causing harm might be greatly increased. Consider the truck attacks in Nice in 2016 and Jerusalem in 2017. Instead of such terrible but isolated events, suppose large trucks in large numbers could be remotely hijacked and used as weapons. The Internet of things makes that sort of event plausible. Even smart refrigerators have been used in denial of service attacks.[25]

Admiral Mike Rogers, director of America's National Security Agency, asked in 2016, "What happens when non-state actors stop viewing the internet, the World Wide Web, as a communication mechanism, as a mechanism to coordinate, as a mechanism to generate revenue, as a mechanism to spread their ideology and recruit, and they start viewing it as a weapon system?"[26] That question is yet to be answered.

---

[25] Patrick Tucker, "How Will Terrorists Use the Internet of Things?," *Defense One*, September 8, 2016, www.defenseone.com/technology/2016/09/how-will-terrorists-use-internet-things-justice-department-trying-figure-out/131381/ [accessed September 9, 2016].

[26] Patrick Tucker and Caroline Houck, "Someone Weaponized the Internet of Things," *Defense One*, October 22, 2016, www.defenseone.com/threats/2016/10/someone-weaponized-internet-things/132553/ [accessed October 23, 2016].

LEGAL AND ETHICAL ISSUES

Do terrorists have rights? The answer is a definitive "yes and no." Every country has laws under which those involved in terrorism – from the planning stages to an actual attack – can be charged and tried in court like any other criminal. But when fighters for organizations such as Al Qaeda and IS are captured in the field, should they be treated as prisoners of war (the undeclared "war on terrorism"), or something else? According to the US government, Al Qaeda and the Taliban are nonstate actors and not parties to the Geneva Conventions, and so their fighters captured in Afghanistan have been considered "unlawful combatants" and not entitled to the conventions' protections.[27] Some of these prisoners had to endure treatment that at times amounted to torture at Abu Ghraib, Guantanamo, and scattered "black sites." Some who were held for years were extremely dangerous, but others could safely have been released.

Terrorism, especially attacks that might involve WMD, has changed the nature of law and war. When the Japanese attacked Pearl Harbor in 1941, the United States immediately responded with a declaration of war and began combat operations. The target was Japan and its military, and the goal was to drive Japan out of territory it had seized and force it to surrender. When the Soviet Union deployed nuclear weapons to Cuba in 1962, the magnitude of the threat and the brief time it would take for those weapons to strike the American mainland led President Kennedy to order a preemptive naval "quarantine" of Cuba – essentially a blockade, which is an act of war – without first going to Congress. By 2001, in the aftermath of the 9/11 attacks and fear that WMD could be smuggled into the United States, Kennedy's preemption gave way to the concept of *preventive* warfare. Vice President Dick Cheney endorsed a doctrine that if there was even a 1 percent chance of terrorists

---

[27] Rosa Brooks, *How Everything Became War and the Military Became Everything* (New York: Simon and Schuster, 2016), 56.

acquiring such weapons, the United States must treat the acquisition as a certainty and act accordingly. Cheney said, "It's not about our analysis or finding a preponderance of evidence. It's about our response."[28]

Under this doctrine, any nation that adopted it could go to war based on the slimmest shreds of evidence – the 1 percent chance. Supporters of Cheney's concept can argue that terrorism and the portability of WMD have so changed the nature of conflict that centuries-old justifications for war have become obsolete. Opponents of the Cheney doctrine can argue that this is too flimsy a rationale – that a higher level of certainty must be reached before unleashing the horrors of war. The debate goes on.

This is just one of the legal and moral issues that continue to evolve during the age of terrorism. It can be argued that this is a victory of sorts for terrorists; they are forcing society to alter its standards for engaging in conflict, making the path to war easier to traverse. This has been accompanied by development of new weaponry that further removes disincentives to war because the likelihood of sustaining casualties while inflicting them on an enemy has been greatly reduced. Today, the leaders of a few militarily advanced countries can say about killing their enemies, "Let the robots do it!"

The "robots" most often used so far are drones, controlled from bases thousands of miles from where they patrol and strike. For US military planners, Afghanistan, Iraq, and Syria are deemed areas of "active hostilities," where US military involvement was widely known. But President Obama also authorized nearly 500 drone strikes in Pakistan, Yemen, Libya, and Somalia. Figures of civilian casualties in drone attacks differ widely between the numbers released by the US government and those compiled by NGOs. In 2013, Obama ordered that drone pilots, before firing, have "near certainty" that

---

[28] Ron Suskind, *The One Percent Doctrine* (New York: Simon and Schuster, 2006), 62.

noncombatants would not be harmed.[29] But how "near" to certainty is required?

Drones offer an easy way to slide into conflict with physical, if not moral, impunity. Even if a drone is shot down, the faraway pilot will be unhurt. This removes an important consideration that military commanders have always had to address before entering combat: "How many losses will my side sustain?" Some commanders have cared less than others about this, but when the answer is "zero," even the most cautious commander is likely to edge closer to ordering an attack. Drone strikes in the countries mentioned in the preceding text have targeted terrorist groups, and this is likely to continue as a key tactic in countering terrorism, but already terrorists have displayed enough understanding of their foes' rules of engagement to situate themselves whenever possible so close to civilians that drone and missile attacks might be forestalled. And it didn't take long for IS to begin using armed drones.

Drone warfare is an early manifestation of what will be a growing role for robotic combat. Robots are being used in scouting and bomb disposal, and the robotic infantry soldier may appear on the battlefields of the near future. Some of the ethical aspects of command will be transformed as a result.

The change in warfare is just one example of the altered norms that have accompanied the rise of terrorism. Ethical issues are not, however, limited to distant battlefields. In a society that has become increasingly dependent on twenty-first-century communication technologies, balancing an individual's right to privacy and the larger community's right to security is a complex task.

In the United States, this issue is at the heart of the debate about the extent to which the government should be allowed to review a person's Internet activity. At the FBI's request in 2016, Congress considered legislation to allow the bureau to obtain "electronic communication transactional records" by using a form of subpoena called a

---

[29] "The Queen and Her Drones," *Economist*, July 9, 2016, 21.

national security letter (NSL). An NSL is not a search warrant and does not require a judge's approval. It can be issued by the agent in charge of an FBI field office and can require tech firms to provide browsing and e-mail histories, although not the user's actual e-mail content or what was viewed when visiting a particular website.

As Ellen Nakashima reported, this information "could reveal details about a person's political affiliation, medical conditions, religion, and movements throughout the day." An NSL includes a gag order, so an Internet service provider may not inform the individual that the government is reviewing her or his records.[30] The FBI-backed measure lost narrowly in a US Senate vote in June 2016, but civil liberties groups warned that it might be resurrected. An alternative proposal would require law enforcement to get a warrant for any e-mail content it wished to access. In January 2017, a measure that would have allowed the FBI greater access to a person's e-mail was dropped from an intelligence authorization bill by a US Senate committee.[31]

As with weaponry, investigative tools have become more sophisticated, and that can produce ethical dilemmas. Drones make military operations safer (for those who have them), and thus using them becomes more tempting. Electronic snooping is likewise easier and more likely to take place; between 2006 and 2016, the FBI issued more than 300,000 NSLs.[32] At some point, the public will need to make its views about these matters known. Although the government can expect great leeway if it brands its action as "counterterrorism," those measures can eat away at fundamental freedoms. The "cure" might be worse than the malady.

Another example of the difficulty in balancing the terrorism prevention and privacy protection can be seen in the British

[30] Ellen Nakashima, "FBI Wants Access to Internet Browser History without a Warrant in Terrorism and Spy Cases," *Washington Post*, June 6, 2016.

[31] Zack Whittaker, "Intelligence Bill Drops FBI Bid to Read Americans' Browser History, Email Records," *ZDNet*, January 18, 2017, www.zdnet.com/article/fbi-bid-for-americans-browsing-email-records-pulled-from-intelligence-bill/ [accessed January 19, 2017].

[32] Nakashima, "FBI Wants Access."

government's "Prevent" program (discussed in another context in Chapter 4). This is an effort to divert young people judged to be vulnerable to radicalization. It creates a legal duty for schools, hospitals, social services agencies, and other institutions to notify authorities about "extremist behavior." Teachers are given Arabic dictionaries so they can recognize words such as *kaffir*, a pejorative term for non-Muslims, and *rafidah*, meaning "rejectionists," a derogatory word referring to Shiite Muslims. Some schools have also installed monitoring devices on their computers so they can track the material students view online. Those young people flagged by the program are is screened by police and may be asked to participate in deradicalization counseling. This is voluntary, because at this stage these people are judged by the government to be "precriminal." During the first half of 2015, more than 3,200 referrals were made.[33]

"Prevent" has been criticized as fostering racial and religious profiling. It targets the Muslim community under the assumption that this is the place to look for "extremist behavior." It also sanctions spying on students' computer use and eavesdropping on their conversations. Preventing radicalization is important, but at what point do such measures cross the line into inappropriate invasion of privacy? As with the NSL example in the United States, to what extent does "counterterrorism" justify intrusions into areas that may be none of the government's business?

Mammoth, technology-rich superagencies, such as America's National Security Agency, can watch individuals to a degree that would astonish even George Orwell. Monitoring phone calls, e-mails, and physical location becomes only easier as people rely ever more on the electronic tools that have become so much a part of everyday life. While the capacity for such intrusion grows, and assuming that the threat of terrorism does not significantly diminish, the public must decide how committed it is to protecting fundamental privacy.

---

[33] Kimiko de Freytas-Tamura, "British Effort to Identify Potential Radicals Spurs Debate over Profiling," *New York Times*, February 9, 2016.

In some ways, these matters related to societal norms represent a victory for extremists in that they have forced retreats from often hard-won standards in the relationship between the individual and government. One need not be a libertarian to worry about government overreach, which is made far easier when wrapped in the claim of being a response to terrorism. Standards can be designed that preserve rights while still allowing effective measures to counter the dangers posed by terrorism. The problem, however, is that when people are frightened they may be quick to surrender (or at least allow abridging of) rights that they expect to retrieve "later," after necessary antiterrorism steps have been taken. When new laws are labeled as "patriotic" or "vigilant," their long-term effects might not be pondered. "Later" might never come. This is one of the lasting costs incurred during the terrorism era.

ISLAM'S ROLE

It is politically correct to separate concerns about terrorism from discussions about Islam, but it is naïve to make that separation absolute. Although only a tiny fraction of the world's 1.6 billion Muslims participate in or even passively endorse terrorist activity, in the minds of many who live in the non-Muslim world, the linkage exists. But the real connection is in victimization; most of the people killed in terrorist attacks are Muslims.

For these reasons, among others, Islam's global prospects are relevant when considering the future of terrorism. As with any minority group, especially one with a disproportionately large percentage of new arrivals, adjusting to a new home takes time ... and the new home also takes time to adjust to its newcomers. With millions of Arab refugees – most of whom are Muslim – on the move from conflict in their homelands, the percentages of Muslim residents in some non-Muslim European countries will grow substantially. It is important to remember that many of these may never return to their original homes; many cities in Syria, for example, are unlikely to be habitable, much less welcoming, for years to come.

Many of the refugees have found temporary homes in other Muslim countries – primarily Turkey, Jordan, and Lebanon – but, legally or not, some will move westward toward Europe's presumably better economic prospects.

They should not expect to be warmly received. A 2016 Pew Research Center survey conducted in ten EU nations found that "the refugee crisis and the threat of terrorism are very much related to one another in the minds of many Europeans. In eight of the ten European nations surveyed, half or more believe incoming refugees increase the likelihood of terrorism in their country." The survey also found worries about the economic impact of the influx of newcomers. Further, general attitudes toward Muslims were negative among 35 percent or more of the respondents in seven of the countries, although these views fluctuated between 2014 and 2016.[34] The threat of terrorism provides a convenient cloak of legitimacy to xenophobia. The anti-refugee policies adopted by the Trump administration is an example of this.

A related issue concerns how Islam is perceived by Muslims. Asma Lamrabet wrote that within the Muslim world there is "refusal of any reformist reading of Islamic tradition and the absence of a counter-narrative to radical religious rhetoric ... It must be recognized that the extremist discourse gets its raw material from a literal Islamic narrative rooted in an outdated Islamic body of knowledge perceived to be sacred. This ideology seeks to radicalize through a religious narrative speaking to the most vulnerable."[35]

As with the internal affairs of any religion, this is a matter that must be solved from within. Many observers have argued that rather than a "clash of civilizations" between the Muslim and non-Muslim worlds, there is a "clash of Islams." Not just among Sunni, Shia, Sufi, and other forms of the religion, but also among Muslim

[34] Richard Wike, Bruce Stokes, and Katie Simmons, "Europeans Fear Wave of Refugees Will Mean More Terrorism, Fewer Jobs," Pew Research Center, July 11, 2016, www.pewglobal.org/2016/07/11/europeans-fear-wave-of-refugees-will-mean-more-terrorism-fewer-jobs/ [accessed August 1, 2016].

[35] Asma Lamrabet, "How to Defeat Radicalism," World Today, April/May 2016, 35.

conservatives, progressives, and those in between. Although the results of this struggle will have effects beyond the *ummah*, many Muslims rightly resent prescriptions from outsiders about how to "fix" their religion.

That is not to say that non-Muslims are disengaged from shaping perceptions of Islam. One of the principal arguments advanced by IS has been that Muslims are widely vilified and, as noted by Jad Melki and May Jabado, "the caliphate is an alternative world where the Muslim is desired and successful, rather than being alienated and considered a nuisance, a message perpetuated by many rightwing Western politicians."[36]

The idea that much of the world is uncaring, at best, about Muslims has been reinforced by apparent nonchalance about so many terrorist victims being other Muslims. When an attack kills Western innocents in Paris, Brussels, or Orlando, social media quickly become crowded with images of flags and other symbols from the countries where the attack took place. But when the attack occurs in Baghdad or Istanbul, outsiders seem to take little notice. Perhaps this is due to "Middle East fatigue," a feeling that the region is perpetually violent and so even horrendous attacks on civilians merit no special notice. But, again, this serves as reinforcement for the case that Muslims must reject the outside world because it rejects them.[37]

THE VALUE OF PUBLIC DIPLOMACY

For many, the instinctive response to terrorism – particularly when terrorists operate on as large a scale and as ferociously as IS has done – is fiercely kinetic. Unleash the SEALs, the drones, the stealth bombers ... whatever the military arsenal has available. Some Western politicians have even implied they would use nuclear weapons, to make Middle Eastern deserts "glow in the dark."

---

[36] Jad Melki and May Jabado, "Mediated Public Diplomacy of the Islamic State in Iraq and Syria: The Synergistic Use of Terrorism, Social Media, and Branding," *Media and Communication* 4 (2), 2016, 100.

[37] Anne Barnard, "After Attacks on Muslims, Many Ask: Where Is the Outpouring?," *New York Times*, July 5, 2016.

Aggressive posturing is, by itself, a painless way to address terrorism, although it has little practical effect. And without doubt, terrorist groups – whether Al Qaeda in Afghanistan in 2001 or IS in Syria and Iraq more recently – must be confronted militarily. But over the long term, prevention rather than just post facto reaction is essential. Unless terrorists' appeal to prospective recruits and other supporters can be undermined, terrorism will be a perpetual and increasingly deadly plague.

As discussed in earlier chapters, part of the counterterrorism effort is focused on messaging and countermessaging, with heavy reliance on social media. Credibility is crucial to such work, and so governments' fingerprints on online products should be as invisible as possible.

An entirely different dimension of terrorism prevention is needed for the long haul: permanent, institutionalized programs designed to alter the sociopolitical terrain that terrorist groups have found so fertile. These efforts should be directed at large swathes of the publics in the many places around the globe where terrorism has already taken root or might yet develop. This is a role for public diplomacy.

While traditional diplomacy is a government–government relationship, public diplomacy involves reaching out directly to foreign publics. That is a simple definition; the universe of public diplomacy practitioners is populated by governments, NGOs, educational and cultural institutions, private companies, and even individuals. But whoever the players may be, a nation when using public diplomacy employs "soft power" – attraction rather than coercion – to advance its interests. This latter point is important: *Public diplomacy is a tool to advance national interests.* It must be built on more than altruism and generosity, and must be driven by the quest to achieve policy goals. Just being "nice" is not part of this equation.

To be successful, public diplomacy should be designed to bring about incremental change in attitudes and behavior, and it should be proactive rather than reactive. It is not a good crisis–response option, which is one reason that many public diplomacy programs created to respond to terrorism after the fact have been unable to gain enough traction to be measurably effective.

Among the most successful public diplomacy efforts over the years has been the British Council's English language training, which is in demand throughout the world. British Council research has found that once people know the language, they are more favorably disposed toward the United Kingdom. For the new English speakers, native English speakers seem less "foreign," and this can influence attitudes about culture and governments.[38]

Another long-term public diplomacy program is the Peace Corps, a US project created by President John F. Kennedy in 1961 and still running today. As of 2015, 220,000 Peace Corps volunteers had served in 140 countries, mostly in Africa and Latin America.[39] Peace Corps volunteers working in communities throughout the world offer personalized representation of American character and help make the United States less of an abstract, and often negatively perceived, presence.

Teaching English and digging wells might seem far removed from dealing with terrorists, but at some point terrorism leaves the grand geopolitical realm and comes down to individuals deciding that they are so angry or frustrated with their lives or the state of the world more broadly that they can be swayed by terrorists' claims that there is an enemy responsible for this state of affairs and that they should fight that enemy. If, however, the people to whom these recruitment advances are directed at have had personal contact with a British Council language instructor or a Peace Corps volunteer, they may have a basis for resisting the demonizing that is part of terrorists' sales pitch.

An example (among many) of the "think smaller" public diplomacy approach is the work of a US-based NGO, impl.project,

---

[38] British Council, *The English Effect*, www.britishcouncil.org/sites/default/files/ english-effect-report-v2.pdf [accessed February 27, 2016].

[39] www.peacecorps.gov/fastfacts [accessed May 22, 2016].

in Mindanao, Philippines. This area was home to elements of Bangsamoro Islamic Liberation Fighters and Moro Islamic Liberation Front, some of which had declared allegiance to IS. Young men in Barira, a farming village, were being pulled out of school by parents to work on their farms, which were failing partly because they lacked essential agricultural equipment. Faced with discouraging prospects, many of the young men became addicted to methamphetamines and began stealing livestock to support their habit. With farming apparently no longer an option, they faced a choice of joining the militia of a local warlord, who would supply them with meth, or join aspiring IS fighters to search for redemption through martyrdom.

When impl.project workers surveyed the community, residents cited "lack of livelihood" as their number one problem. The NGO's response was to help develop an agricultural co-op, teach residents basic economic skills, and encourage young people to return to school. To support the farmers, impl.project purchased a solar dryer for their crops for US$6,000.[40]

In the grand scheme of things, this microapproach might seem insignificant, and it is difficult to prove that this NGO's efforts made a difference in dampening proextremist sentiment among the young men of Barira. Generally, financial stability is not an antidote for extremism's appeal. But such projects, multiplied a thousand-fold, might help make extremist activity less alluring because the targets of recruitment would decide that their lives, although far from ideal, have a chance to become better. Believing that, they might see that they have better things to do than engage with terrorists.

The US State Department has recognized that aid programs are an essential part of the public diplomacy aspects of dealing with terrorism's roots. A State Department report issued in May 2016 stated,

---

[40] Justin Richmond and Ryan B. Greer, "To Beat ISIS, We Must Think Smaller," *Defense One*, May 12, 2016, www.defenseone.com/ideas/2016/05/beat-isis-we-must-think-smaller/128243 [accessed May 13, 2016]; "Preventing Violent Extremism: Mindanao, Philippines," impl.project policy brief, April 2016, http://implproject.org/wp-content/uploads/2016/04/impl_Philippines_Policy_Brief.pdf [accessed June 1, 2016].

"In many environments where the risk of violent extremism is high, development has failed to take root, governance is weak, access to education and training is limited, economic opportunities are few, and unemployment is high."[41]

For the United States, this underscores the need for more collaboration between State Department and USAID program planners to undercut extremists' efforts. But it also triggers some alarm bells. First, new joint programs could produce more layers of bureaucracy that might impair the nimbleness required in effective counterextremism work. Also, it is important that new efforts be adequately funded. The State Department report cited a promising project in East Africa, for example, but stated that only US$19 million in resources would be available for it. East Africa, with the strong presence of Al Shabaab and IS, could well become an even more poisonous center of terrorism, and shortchanging preventive measures might prove self-defeating.[42]

Evidence of aid projects' influence on the opinions of those whose countries receive the aid has been collected only sporadically. A study conducted in Bangladesh that gave information about US aid programs to people considered to be anti-American found that "some people who otherwise would have said that the United States has a large, negative influence on Bangladesh dramatically change their opinion in the face of information about U.S. foreign assistance."[43]

The projects described here illustrate the more holistic approach being endorsed by those who want to counter violent extremism. Sometimes this is a grudging embrace; administrative

---

[41] "Department of State and USAID Joint Strategy on Countering Violent Extremism," May 2016, www.state.gov/documents/organization/257913.pdf [accessed June 1, 2016].

[42] Philip Seib, "An Important CVE Step from the State Department," *Huffington Post*, May 26, 2016, www.huffingtonpost.com/philip-seib/an-important-cve-step-fro_b_10147068.html [accessed May 26, 2016].

[43] Simone Dietrich and Matthew S. Winters, "Foreign Aid Can Help Combat Anti-Western Sentiment in Bangladesh," *Washington Post*, July 2, 2016, www .washingtonpost.com/news/monkey-cage/wp/2016/07/02/foreign-aid-can-help-combat-anti-western-sentiment-in-bangladesh/ [accessed July 3, 2016].

turf and funding might need to be surrendered or shared, and that is always an agonizing process for government bureaucracies. Progress, however, is progress, and perhaps as recognition grows that the fight against terrorism will be a lengthy one, cooperation in these efforts will become more common.

As part of the long-range view, public diplomacy planners should be particularly cognizant of the interests and needs of young people. This is part of the strategy of turning off the recruiting faucet that IS and other terrorist groups rely on. A 2016 Chatham House report cited the alienation growing out of feelings of disempowerment and stressed the need for "provision of platforms for young people to express their views."[44]

This ties into the many issues related to how the rise of new media affects public diplomacy. The connectivity provided, especially by social media, empowers publics in unprecedented ways, or at least creates aspirations to empowerment. These publics, individually and collectively, expect to be listened to and to participate in conversations that were formerly dominated by corporate information providers and governments. Instead of being a passive "audience" receiving information through one-way communication, individuals can respond to the sources of information. They can also build their own online communities of interest within which ideas – positive and negative – can be exchanged. In some circumstances, that can be used to stimulate political mobilization, which also can be positive or negative.

If social media venues are filled with Muslims complaining about being discriminated against and being unable to find jobs or access social services, the task of extremist recruiters becomes much easier. If, by contrast, social media conversations focus on opportunity, then violence and martyrdom are likely to seem pointless.

---

[44] Claire Spencer and Saad Aldouri, "Young Arab Voices: Moving Youth Policy from Debate into Action," Chatham House Research Paper, May 2016, 2, www.chathamhouse.org/sites/files/chathamhouse/publications/research/2016-05-13-young-arab-voices-spencer-aldouri.pdf [accessed June 20, 2016].

Among those who have demonstrated their understanding of this communication environment and the context it provides for political discussions are the media gurus of IS and other terrorist groups. As discussed in Chapter 4, IS uses social media for recruitment on several levels – delivering information to a large audience and courting individuals through intensive back-and-forth messaging. To counter this, an array of governments and antiterrorist organizations have used online media in efforts to undercut terrorists' appeal. But over the long term, such merely reactive public diplomacy will not be enough. New mechanisms need to be created to allow publics to directly engage with those governments and other institutions that terrorists vilify.

Again, an example of a microproject may point the way toward successful broader programs. TechGirls is an exchange program that in 2016 brought to the United States twenty-seven teenage girls from Algeria, Egypt, Jordan, Morocco, Palestine, and Tunisia to participate in three weeks of training in the STEM fields – science, technology, engineering, and mathematics. In addition to classroom training, they received mentoring from tech industry leaders. Admittedly, twenty-seven is not a large number, but there are more than 100 alumnae of the program and they have trained more than 2,300 other teenage girls in their home countries.[45] Over the years, that growth can have greater impact.

TechGirls was conceived partly to offer new opportunities to young women, but it also is a way to help a wider array of young people in the Middle East to recognize that the future can hold alternatives to hopelessness, and that life can be used more productively than by killing others or sacrificing yourself. This and similar programs have the potential to develop a talented and hopeful constituency well disposed toward the country that provided their

---

[45] "TechGirls from the Middle East and North Africa Invest in STEM Futures," Office of the Spokesperson, US Department of State, July 11, 2016, www .state.gov/r/pa/prs/ps/2016/07/259562.htm [accessed July 14, 2016].

training and further opportunities. This is what public diplomacy is supposed to do.

WHO IS "WINNING"?

In July 2016, a *Washington Post* article was headlined, "Inside ISIS: Quietly Preparing for the Loss of the 'Caliphate.'" The article cited "a longtime IS operative," interviewed online with a promise of anonymity, who said, "While we see our core structure in Iraq and Syria under attack, we have been able to expand and have shifted some of our command, media, and wealth structure to different countries." He added that IS was telling prospective recruits not to come to Iraq or Syria, but "to stay in their countries and wait to do something there."[46] This echoed the comment several months earlier of IS spokesman Abu Muhammad al-Adnani: "The smallest action you do in their heartland is better and more enduring to us than what you would [do] if you were with us."[47]

Clearly, the situation on the ground in Iraq and Syria had changed dramatically since the IS sweep that began in summer 2014, highlighted by the seizure of Mosul. When it had to deal only with the Baghdad government's army in Iraq and an array of Syrian opponents in that country, IS could take and hold territory. But with Kurdish forces pushing them from one direction, rejuvenated Iraqi troops from another, and major powers pounding them with air strikes (as well as putting some of their own troops on the ground), IS found itself overmatched and altered some of its tactics. IS increased its suicide attacks from fifty to sixty attributed to it in November 2015 to 112 in March 2016. Although some observers said this reflected desperation, others said it was merely a shift in response to the changing overall military situation.[48]

---

[46] Joby Warrick and Souad Mekhennet, "Inside ISIS: Quietly Preparing for the Loss of the 'Caliphate,'" *Washington Post*, July 12, 2016.

[47] "Islamic Stateless?," *Economist*, July 9, 2016, 39.

[48] Hassan Hassan, "Is the Islamic State Unstoppable?," *New York Times*, July 9, 2016.

This is not a conventional conflict, and losing physical territory does not mean defeat. For one thing, pushing IS out of certain places does not mean that they cannot return; consider the history of IS predecessor Al Qaeda in Iraq, which was driven underground for several years before re-emerging as the far stronger IS. Also, the Taliban in Afghanistan were thrashed by US forces in 2001, but were still viable (and then some) as 2017 began.

The long-term resilience of IS will be determined not just by its battleground competence or the ferocity of its terror attacks, but also by the sustained fervor of its constituency. Mark Juergensmeyer wrote of this: "The young people who were lured to this network and who maintain it came with a variety of motives. Perhaps the strongest was the desire to be involved in a great war, a cosmic struggle that allowed them to play out all their computer game fantasies of Warcraft, valor, and gore. But some also came out of a sense of history and piety, a conviction that they were laying their lives on the line for something of transcendent importance for Islamic civilization ... Indeed, the passion of belonging to the ISIS cyber community might even intensify in the period after the fall of territorial control. Perhaps nothing brings together a community as the sense of being under siege and needing to band together for strength."[49]

Juergenmeyer's observation makes sense, but it depends on the actual cohesion of the "community" he described. This depends on the nature of virtual connectivity. He notes that "Individuals can be comforted by the fact that even though their horrible actions are condemned by most people, including most Muslims, around the globe, their comrades in the online communities forged through Internet connections will digitally applaud their crimes."[50] How sustaining is "digital applause"? Can this virtual community – from which it is so easy to walk away – give its members the sense of belonging and permanence that is more easily fashioned in a real, on-the-ground

---

[49] Mark Juergensmeyer, "How ISIS Will End," *Cairo Review of Global Affairs* 22, Summer 2016, 59–60.
[50] Ibid., 61.

community? As the era of virtual communities and virtual states proceeds, answers to such questions may take shape.

Sometimes overlooked when contemplating IS's future is that IS is, according to Andrew Liepman and Colin Clarke, an ideology: "What it represents is the embodiment of Salafi jihadism and all of its undercurrents – anti-American, anti-Jewish, and, of course, anti-Shia."[51] That said, continued Liepman and Clarke, it is important to remember "what the Islamic state is not: It is not an existential threat on the order of the challenge the United States faced during the Cold War. It is not a nuclear-armed nation-state like the Soviet Union, nor is it a near-peer adversary, trained and equipped for conventional military operations like China, Iran, or North Korea."[52] This perspective is sometimes difficult to maintain, particularly after IS launches one of its grisly attacks, but the threat terrorism poses might never be wholly eradicated. It must be contained, which is doable, but unless the level of terrorist activity escalates to the use of WMD, it is manageable. (Those of us who lived through the 1962 Cuban Missile Crisis may remember what facing a true existential threat is like.) Realistic assessment of the threat level is crucial on the home front, as the extent of the threat may affect the level of protection accorded to privacy and other civil liberties.

Aside from the United States, the Iraqi and Kurdish militaries, and a few other enemies, such as Iran, perhaps the biggest extended challenge IS faces is from Al Qaeda, which competes with IS for the loyalty of groups such as Boko Haram. If IS can no longer claim a physical caliphate and is reduced to telling its followers to just "blow up things at home," it might become seen as merely another violent group without any particular appeal. Al Qaeda, however, has established its brand over twenty years, and although it has never seized large swathes of territory, as IS has, it retains the credibility it

---

[51] Andrew Liepman and Colin P. Clarke, "Demystifying the Islamic State," *RAND Blog*, August 23, 2016, 2, www.rand.org/blog/2016/08/demystifying-the-islamic-state.html [accessed August 27, 2016].

[52] Ibid., 3.

earned in its attacks on New York, Washington, London, Madrid, and elsewhere. As noted earlier, Al Qaeda has been rebuilding, more or less quietly. How it might try to reassert itself is unpredictable, but the competition between it and IS could be exceptionally bloody if each tries to outdo the other in headline-grabbing tactics. If, however, they forge an alliance, the potential for violent ramifications would be hard to calculate.

Should IS lose the territory it once held and the caliphate becomes even more virtual rather than physical, it will be even more dependent on its online presence. Here, as well, anti-IS governments have found increasing success. With growing emphasis on Arabic language countermessaging and with expanded content, counterterrorism efforts have helped to reportedly cut the number of IS followers on Twitter and established a 6:1 ratio of anti-IS to pro-IS online material.[53] This might be an overly optimistic assessment. IS has alternatives to Twitter for its communications, such as the earlier mentioned dark web and Telegram. IS messaging may have become less visible, but that does not mean that it is gone.

Whatever the messaging balance, outreach must continue to the young people whom extremist groups seek to recruit, especially those who have endured years of violence and being uprooted from their homes. The next generation of potential terrorists is out there, and a big question is, who can get to them first and most convincingly?

On a larger scale, the badly broken political systems of the Arab world will, unless repaired, continue to give rise to extremist groups. As Aaron David Miller observed, "[T]he lack of effective leadership and representative institutions, and the pestilence of bad or no governance," have created ample opportunities for extremists to build constituencies.[54] Miller's view was echoed by former Egyptian foreign

---

[53] "ISIL Twitter Traffic Down by Nearly Half," *National* (Abu Dhabi), July 10, 2016, www.thenational.ae/world/middle-east/isil-twitter-traffic-down-by-nearly-half [accessed July 12, 2016].

[54] Aaron David Miller, "The Problem with ISIS," *Real Clear World*, February 18, 2016, www.realclearworld.com/blog/2016/02/the_problem_with_isis_111713 .html [accessed February 24, 2016].

minister Nabil Fahmy, who wrote that "terrorism in the Middle East is a direct derivative of the breakdown of the social contract and the absence of effective state institutions."[55]

To some extent, this current situation can be traced back to the failure of the "Arab spring" of 2011 to bring about broad and lasting change. Robert Worth wrote: "The protestors of 2011 had dreamed of building new countries that would confer genuine citizenship and something more: *karama*, dignity, the rallying cry of all the uprisings. When that dream failed them, many gave way to apathy or despair, or even nostalgia for the old regimes they had assailed. But some ran headlong into the seventh century in search of the same prize. They wanted something they had heard about and imagined all their lives but never really known: a *dawla* [nation] that would not melt into air beneath their feet, a place they could call their own, a state that shielded its subjects from humiliation and despair."[56]

Outsider nations that want to damage terrorism's long-term prospects should recognize this aspect of political psychology and focus even more on encouraging growth of civil society and social justice in nations where extremists have found fertile ground for recruiting. Creative approaches to prevention of extremist violence must be designed within a well-understood political context, such as that which Worth describes.

At the heart of such efforts must be grassroots organizing; US Deputy Secretary of State Anthony Blinken referred to the need to "amplify locally credible voices" and cited the work of mayors and civic volunteers in Senegal, Mali, Tajikistan, and Belgium who have labored within their own communities to defuse potential radicalization of young people.[57] Similarly, the National Counterterrorism

---

[55] Nabil Fahmy, "A Call for Arab Diplomacy," *Cairo Review of Global Affairs* 21, Spring 2016, 81, www.thecairoreview.com/essays/a-call-for-arab-diplomacy/ [accessed July 1, 2016].

[56] Worth, *A Rage for Order*, 233–4.

[57] Anthony J. Blinken, "New Frameworks for Countering Terrorism and Violent Extremism," remarks at the Brookings Institution, February 16, 2016, www.state.gov/s/d/2016d/252547.htm [accessed March 1, 2016].

Center notes successful programs in places such as Lewiston, Maine, which has 40,000 residents of whom 6,000 are Somalis and other immigrants from conflict zones. Relying on community policing and a network of schools and community service organizations, Lewiston has sought to prevent its newcomers from becoming socially isolated.[58]

Such projects can become complicated, particularly when apparent conflicts of interest arise. Social workers, for example, who devote their professional efforts to protecting children may not want to be informers or contribute information to a database that will be used in uncertain ways. Another matter that requires further consideration is the role of schools, especially in teaching about religion. Perhaps Islamophobia and Muslims' distrust of non-Muslims could be reduced over the long run if young people were introduced to critical thinking in comparative religion classes.

All of this may be wishful thinking, but common sense leads one to think that social conditions and violent extremism are related, at least in some cases. George Packer's analysis of Tunisia as a source of so many IS fighters noted that the revolution that began in 2011 gave young Tunisians "the freedom to act on their unhappiness. By raising and then frustrating expectations, the revolution created conditions for radicalization to thrive." Education, even higher education, is not in itself the answer, because, as Packer found, "educated Tunisians are twice as likely to be unemployed as uneducated ones because the economy creates so few professional jobs."[59]

In such conditions, frustration abounds, and it can easily lead to anger, which in some cases can lead to violence. That continuum must be disrupted.

Damaging terrorism's roots becomes more difficult when the potential recruits of terrorist organizations perceive that their

[58] "Countering Violent Extremism: A Guide for Practitioners and Analysts," National Counterterrorism Center, May 2014, www.documentcloud.org/documents/1657824-cve-guide.html [accessed June 20, 2014].

[59] George Packer, "Exporting Jihad," *New Yorker*, March 28, 2016, 42.

homelands and especially their religion are the subjects of scorn and worse. The protestations of George W. Bush and Barack Obama that their attacks on terrorists were not attacks on Islam were at least somewhat believable, particularly because terrorists were mostly victimizing Muslims and so had minimal support within the Muslim world. But the immigration policies unveiled by Donald Trump at the beginning of his presidency were, despite half-hearted claims to the contrary, clearly targeting Muslims as Muslims. This involves more than 1.6 billion people and the religion that will be the largest on the planet by 2070. Leaders of IS, Al Qaeda, and other terrorist organizations could not have been more delighted. Trump provided evidence that their claims about Islam being under siege were true. Their task of sustaining their murderous enterprises had just become far easier.

Can terrorism around the world be "defeated," in the sense of being truly eradicated? No. As with racism, misogyny, crime, and other harmful elements of modern life, terrorism can be reduced but not extinguished. Some of the stimuli to hatred, however, can be dampened by neutralizing their principal exponents. This is a broader task than it first might seem. Al Qaeda, IS, Boko Haram, Al Shabaab, and others are the most visible perpetrators, but in the shadows behind them may lurk their sponsors – states that profit from disorder and use nonstate actors to carry out crimes that they don't want to be seen committing themselves.

The struggle between those who endorse and produce terror and those who want terrorism to end will continue indefinitely. This battle cannot be left solely to the combatants; using tools such as social media, the global community must try to drown out the voices urging violence and instead foster discourse based on knowledgeable religious and political tolerance.

More wishful thinking? Perhaps, but such thinking, backed by societal actors ranging from the military to religious communities, is at least a foundation on which to build hope for halting terrorism's evolution. What is the alternative?

Select Bibliography

Albright, Madeleine. *The Mighty and the Almighty: Reflections on America, God, and World Affairs*. New York: Harper Perennial, 2007.

Allison, Graham. *Nuclear Terrorism: The Ultimate Preventable Catastrophe*. New York: Times Books, 2004.

Atwan, Abdel Bari. *Islamic State: The Digital Caliphate*. Oakland: University of California, 2015.

Brooks, Rosa. *How Everything Became War and the Military Became Everything*. New York: Simon and Schuster, 2016.

Bush, George W. *Decision Points*. New York: Broadway Books, 2010.

Byman, Daniel. *The Five Front War: The Better Way to Fight Global Jihad*. Hoboken, NJ: Wiley, 2008.

Habila, Helon. *The Chibok Girls: The Boko Haram Kidnappings and Islamist Militancy in Nigeria*. New York: Columbia Global Reports, 2016.

Hansen, Stig Jarle. *Al-Shabaab in Somalia*. New York: Oxford, 2013.

Harik, Judith Palmer. *Hezbollah: The Changing Face of Terrorism*. London: I.B. Tauris, 2004.

Hoffman, Bruce. *Inside Terrorism*. New York: Columbia University, 1998.

Huntington, Samuel L. *The Clash of Civilizations and the Remaking of World Order*. New York: Simon and Schuster, 1996.

Ibrahim, Raymond (ed.). *The Al Qaeda Reader*. New York: Broadway Books, 2007.

Maalouf, Amin. *The Crusades through Arab Eyes*. New York: Schocken, 1989.

Maalouf, Amin. *In the Name of Identity: Violence and the Need to Belong*. New York: Arcade, 2012.

National Commission on Terrorist Attacks upon the United States. *The 9/11 Commission Report*. New York: Norton, 2004.

Said, Edward. *Orientalism*. New York: Vintage, 2003.

Scheuer, Michael. *Imperial Hubris: Why the West Is Losing the War on Terror*. Dulles, VA: Brassey's, 2004.

Seib, Philip, and Dana Janbek. *Global Terrorism and New Media: The Post-Al Qaeda Generation*. London: Routledge, 2011.

Suskind, Ron. *The One Percent Doctrine: Deep Inside America's Pursuit of Its Enemies since 9/11*. New York: Simon and Schuster, 2006.

Telhami, Shibley. *The World through Arab Eyes*. New York: Basic Books, 2013.

The US Army–Marine Corps Counterinsurgency Field Manual. Chicago: University of Chicago, 2007.

Warrick, Joby. *Black Flags: The Rise of ISIS.* New York: Doubleday, 2015.

Weimann, Gabriel. *Terror on the Internet.* Washington, DC: US Institute of Peace, 2006.

Worth, Robert. *A Rage for Order: The Middle East in Turmoil from Tahrir Square to ISIS.* New York: Farrar, Straus and Giroux, 2016.

Wright, Lawrence. *The Looming Tower: Al Qaeda and the Road to 9/11.* New York: Knopf, 2006.

Wright, Lawrence *The Terror Years: From Al Qaeda to the Islamic State.* New York: Knopf, 2016.

Wright, Robin. *Rock the Casbah: Rage and Rebellion across the Islamic World.* New York: Simon and Schuster, 2011.

Index

Abu Ghraib, 158
Aceh, Indonesia, 70
al-Adnani, Abu Muhammad 103, 172
Afghanistan, 3, 7, 24, 27, 30, 35, 86, 91, 103, 105, 109, 110, 112, 115, 151, 158, 159, 173
Africa Check, 83
African Muslims, 150
African Union Mission in Somalia (AMISOM), 86, 106
Ahmari, Sohrab, 76
Ahrar al-Sham ("Free People of the Levant"), 153
aid programs, 31, 168, 169
airlines' computer reservation systems, 142
airplane hijackings, 76, 88, 111
Ajaka, Nadine, 62
al-Ajmi, Hajjaj, 127
Al Arabiya, 22
Al-Assad, Bashar, 79, 88
Al Bayan, 119
Al Jazeera, 67, 115
Al Manar, 22, 89
Al Neda, 112
alahednews, 89
Albright, Madeleine 64, 65
Algeria, 105, 171
algorithm, 140
Al-Khanssaa Brigade, 99
"All Religion Will Be for Allah," 116
Allison, Graham, 147
Amaq News Agency, 108, 119
Amazon, 136
American Revolution, 85
American Sniper, 122
Amin, Ali, 125
AMISOM. *See* African Union Mission in Somalia
Android, 121
anti-Arab sentiment, 42
anti-Muslim sentiment. *See* Islamophobia
antiquities, 126
Apple, 141, 142
AQAP, 30, 79
AQIM, 78, 81

"Arab spring", 67, 176
Arab uprisings 2011, 4, 57
Arab world, 56
Arabic-language countermessaging, 175
archeological sites, 97
Arquilla, John, 113
As Sahab, 12, 115
Asharq Al-Awsat, 59
Ashton Carter, 138
Asma Lamrabet, 164
Asrar al-Dardashah (Secrets of the Chat), 121
Assad, 152
assassination, 113
assimilation, 43
atrocities, 130
attitudes toward IS, 58
Atwan, Abdel Bari, 52, 93, 97
auctions, 127
Austria, 150
al-Awlaki, Anwar 39, 155

Babu, Dal, 133
Bach-Lombardo, Jordan, 128
"backdoor" access, 141
Baghdad, 165
Al-Baghdadi, Abu Bakr, 26, 90
Bahasa Indonesia, 151
Bakr, Haji, 90
Bali, 28
Bangladesh, 136, 144, 169
Bangsamoro Islamic Liberation Fighters, 168
Barira, 168
Baton Rouge, Louisiana 7
"battlefield of media", 118
BBC, 41, 132
Begin, Menachem, 19
beheading, 102
Beirut, 4, 62
Belgium, 80, 146, 176
Ben Ali, Zine el-Abidine, 67
Benghazi, 81
Berg, Nicholas, 116
Bergen, Peter, 37